Mississippi

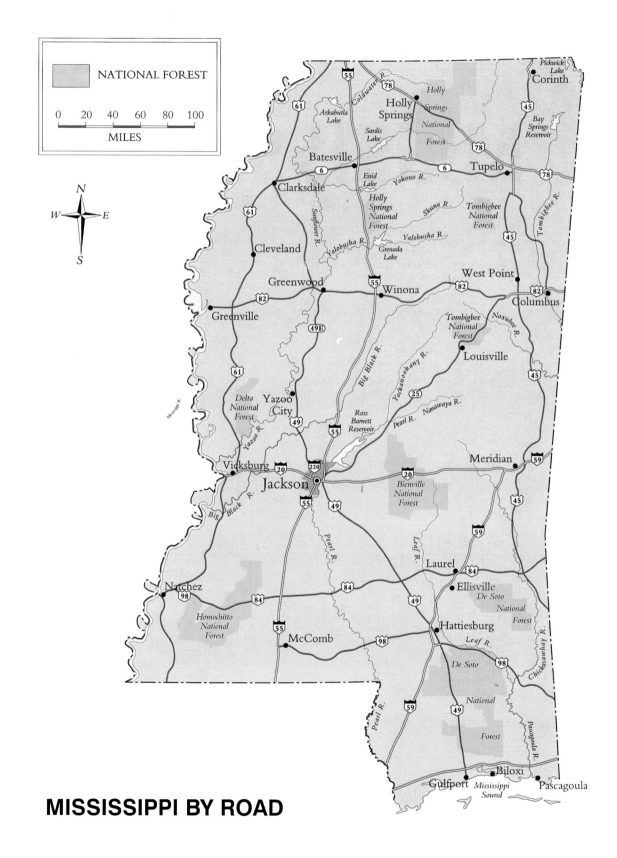

MISSISSIPPI BY ROAD

Celebrate the States

Mississippi

David Shirley and Patricia K. Kummer

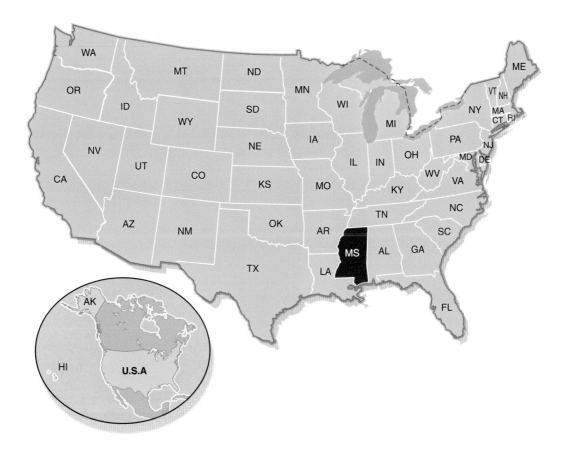

Marshall Cavendish
Benchmark
New York

Marshall Cavendish Benchmark
99 White Plains Road
Tarrytown, NY 10591-9001
www.marshallcavendish.us

All Internet addresses were correct and accurate at the time of printing.

Library of Congress Cataloging-in-Publication Data
Shirley, David, 1955–
Mississippi / by David Shirley. — 2nd ed. / revised by Patricia K. Kummer.
p. cm. — (Celebrate the states)
Summary: "Provides comprehensive information on the geography, history, wildlife, governmental
structure, economy, cultural diversity, peoples, religion, and landmarks of
Mississippi"—Provided by publisher.
Includes bibliographical references and index.
ISBN 978-0-7614-2717-9
1. Mississippi—Juvenile literature. I. Kummer, Patricia K. II. Title. III. Series.
F341.3.S55 2008
976.2—dc22
2007007868

Editor: Christine Florie
Publisher: Michelle Bisson
Art Director: Anahid Hamparian
Series Designer: Adam Mietlowski

Photo research by Connie Gardner

Cover photo by Kelley-Mooney Photography/CORBIS

The photographs in this book are used by permission and through the courtesy of: *Corbis:* Richard Hamilton Smith, back cover, 99; Corbis, 11, 40, 41,119; Charles Krebs, 19; Joe McDonald, 20; Tim Thompson, 21; Darrell Gahn, 22; Matthew Cavanaugh, 26; David G. Houser, 28, 101; E. Boyd Smith, 33; Bettmann, 39, 70, 77, 126; Jim Reed, 47; Kelly Moone Photography, 53, 96, 121; Louis De Luca/Dallas Morning News, 56; Philip Gould, 61, 91, 106, 132; David Butow, 63; Bob Sacha, 65; Neal Preston, 69; Jim Richardson, 87; Phil Schermeister, 88; Vince Stream, 93; Kevin Fleming, 98; Danny Lehman, 104; Richard Cummins, 109; W. Perry Conway, 111(Top); Peter Smiths, 111 (Bottom); Bob Krist, 115; Jeff Christensen, 124; *Alamy:* Bill Barksdale, 8; Jeff Greenberg, 102; *PhotoEdit:* Cathy Melloan Resources, 136; *Getty:* Tom Till, 13; Altrendo Nature, 16; Hulton, 32, 129; Time and Life Pictures, 42, 45; Oliver Strewe, 52; Getty Image News, 54, 84, 120, 128, 133; *NorthWind Picture Archives:* 30, 34, 37, 38; *Dembinsky Photo Associates:* Bill Lea, 14, 17; *Granger:* 43; *Image Works:* David R. Frazier, 18; Andre Jenny, 15; Joseph Sohm 48; Holt Confer, 72; *AP Photo:* Tannen Marcy, 57; Paula Merritt, 59; Kyle Carter, 60; Haley Barbour, 74; WJS, 79; Rogelio Solis, 82; Bill Johnson, 86.

Printed in Malaysia
1 3 5 6 4 2

Contents

A land that appeals to all the senses.

"When I think of Mississippi, I think of down-home cooking, sitting on the porch watching the sun set, southern hospitality, and friendly people."
—Sharon Robinson of Clinton, Mississippi

"In the Delta, most of the world seemed sky. The land was perfectly flat and level, but shimmered like the wing of a lighted dragonfly. It seemed strummed, as though it were an instrument and something had touched it."
—Eudora Welty, Mississippi novelist and short-story writer

No stranger to disaster.

"Katrina ravaged with the mightiest of power and destruction, but the monster storm was no match for the Mississippi spirit. From Biloxi to Batesville, Mississippians were out doing what they do best—helping their neighbors. And in Mississippi, that comes natural."
—Ralph Gordon, writer from Union, Mississippi

The birthplace of the blues.

"The blues is an impulse to keep the painful details and episodes of a brutal experience alive in one's aching consciousness, to finger its jagged grain, and to transcend it."
—Ralph Ellison, novelist and essayist

"The blues ain't nothin' but a good man feelin' bad."
—Traditional blues lyric

A great place to live . . .

"Family, manners, and helping your neighbor will never be out of style. That's probably why Mississippi is called the Hospitality State and why, when adversity hits us, we simply pull up our bootstraps and get on with it."
—Suzanne Cox, a writer in Columbia, Mississippi

"Mississippi is a state with a relaxed atmosphere and warm-hearted people."
—Jason Gardner, Mississippi State University graduate student

. . . to leave, and to long for.

"In my hometown in northeastern Mississippi, there was a real sense of community. Everyone knew everyone else and everyone else's business. My friends and I couldn't wait to get away and we did. Now, we'd like nothing better than to go back in time to that caring, close and, yes, nosey community."
—A former Mississippian now living in Chicago, Illinois

Over and over, Mississippians remark on how friendly, warm, and hospitable their fellow Mississippians are. This has not always been the case. At one time Mississippi was best known for racial inequality. Now, perhaps more than any other state, Mississippi is working hard to correct the mistakes of the past. Sometimes, Mississippi is also known for being ranked as having some of the poorest and least-educated people in the United States. In spite of this, Mississippians have produced some of our nation's most treasured music and literature. After Hurricane Katrina hit Mississippi in August 2005, the whole world saw the real Mississippians—people helping one another and taking care of their own. As the people of Mississippi work together to rebuild after the devastation caused by Hurricane Katrina, they also have an opportunity to create a united state filled with hope and promise for all of its people.

Chapter One

A Small But Beautiful State

When the word *Mississippi* is mentioned, many images come to mind: rich, black soil that produces fluffy, white cotton; live oak trees draped with Spanish moss; tall stands of piney woods; white Gulf Coast beaches that stretch for miles; hot, humid summer days; and, of course, fierce hurricanes. All of this is packed into only 47,914 square miles of land. Indeed, Mississippi is a small but beautiful state.

Mississippi ranks thirty-first in size among the fifty states. It stretches from the Gulf of Mexico in the south to Tennessee in the north. To the east, Mississippi is bordered by Alabama. The state's western border is defined by the smooth, muddy waters of the Mississippi River, with Arkansas across the river in the north and Louisiana in the south.

An abundance of crops, including cotton, grow in Mississippi's fertile soil.

Mississippi is divided into two natural regions, both running north and south for the entire length of the state. In the west is the Mississippi Floodplain, while the eastern Gulf Coastal Plain occupies the rest of the state.

The floodplain covers the flat, narrow stretch of land that runs along the eastern bank of the Mississippi River. "The area around here is so flat," explains a truck driver from Cleveland, "that it feels sometimes like there's nothing but earth and sky. Things seem even flatter in the summer, when it's really hot and the sky gets hazy and heavy. Some days, these old, narrow roads look like a long, straight line that just stretches out forever."

For more than 15,000 years the Mississippi River has frequently flooded, overflowing its banks and dumping rich, black soil from upriver onto vast fields and marshes. The section of the floodplain between the Yazoo River and the Tennessee border is known as the Mississippi Delta. The Delta is one of the nation's most important farming regions, producing huge crops of cotton and soybeans each year.

East of the floodplain is the eastern Gulf Coastal Plain. Unlike the flat, sprawling floodplain, the eastern Gulf Coastal Plain is covered with gentle, rolling hills. With much of the wooded land still undeveloped, the region is known for its tranquil, undisturbed beauty, its abundant wildlife and flowers, and its brilliant, star-filled night skies. "I love these forests in the early morning, before everybody leaves for work," says a construction worker from West Point. "There's no sound anywhere—even the crickets have stopped chirping—and the trees are so still and so silent that you can hear your own heart beat."

Mississippi's southern coastline is guarded from the Gulf of Mexico by a string of barrier islands a few miles offshore. Among these islands are Cat, Deer, East Ship and West Ship, Horn, and Petit Bois.

In the aftermath of Hurricane Katrina these islands lost much of their surface area. As a result, they now offer little protection to Mississippi's coastline. Between the islands and the state's coastline, lie calm, shallow salt waters known as the Mississippi Sound.

A soybean field seems to go on forever in the floodplain region of the state.

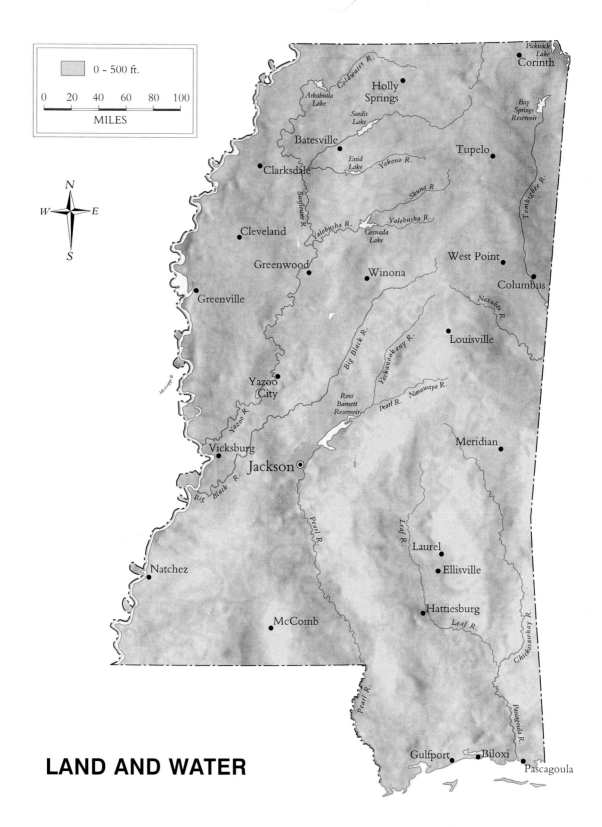

LAND AND WATER

Scale: 0 - 500 ft.

0 20 40 60 80 100
MILES

N
W E
S

Pickwick Lake
Corinth
Coldwater R.
Arkabutla Lake
Holly Springs
Sardis Lake
Bay Springs Reservoir
Batesville
Enid Lake
Yokono R.
Tupelo
Clarksdale
Skuna R.
Tombigbee R.
Sunflower R.
Yalobusha R.
Yalobusha R.
Cleveland
Grenada Lake
West Point
Greenwood
Winona
Columbus
Noxubee R.
Greenville
Louisville
Big Black R.
Yockanookany R.
Mississippi R.
Nanawaya R.
Yazoo City
Ross Barnett Reservoir
Pearl R.
Yazoo R.
Meridian
Vicksburg
Jackson
Big Black R.
Leaf R.
Natchez
Laurel
Ellisville
Pearl R.
Hattiesburg
Chickasawhay R.
McComb
Leaf R.
Pearl R.
Pascagoula R.
Gulfport
Biloxi
Pascagoula

Mississippi is named after the majestic river that forms most of the state's western border. From its elevated shoreline in Natchez or Vicksburg, the Mississippi River is an astonishing sight, even to those who know it well. Its deep, muddy waters stretch out for more than a mile to the green Arkansas hills across the way, cutting and curving sharply as the river stretches south toward the Gulf of Mexico.

The word *Mississippi* was coined from the Muskhogean language and means "big river." In fact, the Mississippi is the largest river in North America. In the western part of the state several major tributaries, including the Big Black River and the Yazoo River, empty into it. Across the rest of the state, a network of rivers and streams flows south toward the Mississippi Sound. The most important of these are the Pearl, Pascagoula, and Tombigbee rivers.

Mississippi also has many lakes and reservoirs. The state's largest bodies of water, which were created by damming rivers, include Pickwick Lake, on

At sunset a dramatic view of the Mississippi River can be seen from Natchez.

the Tennessee River; Arkabutla Lake, on the Coldwater River; Grenada Lake, on the Yalobusha River; and Ross Barnett Reservoir, on the Pearl River. Mississippi is also known for its oxbow lakes. These curved, narrow lakes form when flooding or high water upstream cause a river to change course, leaving the old path behind as a separate, self-enclosed body of water.

Throughout the flatter regions of the state—and in the gullies, ravines, and bottomlands of the hill country—the waters of creeks and streams sometimes overflow into wooded areas, forming swamps and marshes. Gum trees, cypress, and tall oaks often rise out of these still, shallow waters. Altogether, Mississippi has more than 123,000 miles of freshwater streams and lakes covering 225,000 acres of land. The state also has 1,560 square miles of river bottom and swamps.

Freshwater wetlands found along floodplains are referred to as swamps.

A COLORFUL LANDSCAPE

Within Mississippi's borders, nature has painted with an astonishing variety of colors. From north to south, Mississippi's highways and back roads are lined with endless rows of wildflowers. "Nothing is more beautiful than our state's roadsides, especially in the spring" says a merchant in Natchez. "Everywhere you look, you see the magnificent colors of the wildflowers and the trees." Both rural areas and city streets are shaded by a variety of flowering trees and shrubs. The brilliant pink flowers of the azalea and the delicate white blossoms of the dogwood and magnolia are common sights.

The magnolia is an important plant in the state. Mississippi's nickname is "The Magnolia State." The magnolia tree is the state tree, and the flower of this tree is the state flower.

Pink azaleas and live oaks, dripping with Spanish moss, line a country road in Natchez.

Behind the whites, yellows, reds, and purples of Mississippi's flowers is the state's deep green, forested landscape. The state is fortunate to have six national forests. From north to south, they are Holly Springs, Tombigbee, Delta, Homochitto, Bienville, and De Soto national forests. In all, more than 60 percent of Mississippi is covered with forests. The densely wooded hills of the north are covered with a variety of hardwood trees, such as hickory, elm, and blackjack oak. Most of Mississippi's southern forests are filled with row after row of sharp-smelling pine trees—loblolly, longleaf, and slash pines. "Every time that I leave the state," explains a truck driver in the small town of Wiggins, located in the southeastern corner of the state, "the first thing I notice when I get home is the strong, clean smell of those pines. You can say what you want, but the odor of pine trees is as much Mississippi as cotton or magnolias or catfish. It's the one thing that always tells me I'm home."

Dogwood trees in bloom in Holly Springs National Forest

The area's many riverbeds and swamps are lined with cypress, sweet gum, tupelo gum, and live oak trees. Live oaks are also found in Mississippi's towns and cities and grace the grounds of many mansions. The live oak is an unusual tree because it does not drop its leaves in the fall, as do other leaf-bearing trees. That's why it is called a live oak: it stays alive all year and does not become dormant during the winter. From the branches of live oaks, Spanish moss floats in the breeze. This grayish-green plant got its name from French soldiers who said it looked like a Spaniard's beard. Spanish moss is not a moss, but a flowering plant with no roots. The rough bark of the live oaks provides a sure foothold for the Spanish moss. The leathery live oak leaves protect the plant from the hot sun and strong winds. Hanging from live oaks, Spanish moss absorbs all its nutrients from the moisture in Mississippi's humid air.

This live oak is heavy with Spanish moss.

This plant can grow to be 20 feet in length, but the average length is 3 to 4 feet. During the early 1900s Spanish moss was harvested and used as stuffing in furniture and as thread to repair fishing nets.

Kudzu is a strong, green vine that has overrun much of Mississippi as well as other southern states. This fast-growing plant was brought from Japan and introduced into the South during the early 1900s to control soil erosion and as feed for cattle and goats. Mississippi's hot, humid climate helped kudzu grow faster than it normally would—as much as a foot a day. In addition, there were no natural controls for Mississippi's kudzu, as there were in Japan. Now, kudzu is a weed that's out of control, covering anything it comes in contact with—trees, parts of forests, power lines, utility poles, roadway signs, and even buildings. Scientists have been developing weed killers to apply to the kudzu. In 2006 experiments with weed killers on Mississippi kudzu proved successful. Perhaps the kudzu curse will soon be lifted.

A few plants in Mississippi are given federal protected status because they are endangered or threatened. The American chaffseed, Louisiana quillwort, false rosemary, and Southern spicebush are endangered species. Traveler's delight, pondberry, and potato bean are threatened species.

Kudzu vines thrive in the hot and humid climate of Mississippi.

Mississippi's forests and lakes are filled with wild animals. Until early this century, cougars, wild boars, alligators, and bears were widespread in the state's rural regions. Today smaller, less-threatening animals roam the state's fields and forests, including opossums, foxes, rabbits, skunks, and squirrels. With a population of about two million found throughout the state, the white-tailed deer is the state's most common large animal.

Skunks are a common sight in Mississippi.

With the abundance of wild animals and undeveloped land, hunting and fishing are popular pastimes for many Mississippians. The state's principal game birds are quail, duck, and wild turkey. Of all the states, Mississippi has the greatest number of wild turkeys. Sport fishing in Mississippi's Gulf Coast salt water yields redfish, sharks, billfish, speckled trout, white trout, and snapper. The most frequently caught freshwater fish include black bass, bream, perch, crappie, croaker, and catfish.

River frogs make their home in the Mississippi wetlands.

Mississippi is home to several endangered animal species. Among the endangered amphibians are the river frog and the Mississippi gopher tortoise. Pine woods snakes, mimic glass lizards, black pine snakes, hawksbill sea turtles, Kemp's ridley sea turtles, and leatherback sea turtles are some of the state's endangered reptiles. Gulf sturgeon, pallid sturgeon, Alabama shad, crystal darter, Yazoo darter, and bayou darter are some endangered fish. Just about every species of crayfish and several species of mussels in Mississippi are endangered, including the Choctaw rivulet crayfish, Jackson prairie crayfish, Mississippi flatwoods crayfish, pearl blackwater crayfish, mucket mussel, purple wartyback mussel, and Louisiana fatmucket.

Several species of birds are also endangered, including the brown pelican, Mississippi sandhill crane, southeastern snowy plover, yellow rail, southeastern American kestrel, and American oystercatcher. Perhaps the most colorful endangered bird is the red-cockaded woodpecker. This bird, which has a black body covered with tiny white specks, gets its name from the brilliant red stripe at each side of its black cap. Red-cockaded woodpeckers feed and nest exclusively in tall pine trees. The woodpeckers live together in small communities. They take turns guarding their nests and keep a steady stream of sap flowing from the holes that they bore around the nests. It's easy to spot the woodpeckers' nesting area from the huge sap stains on the tree trunks.

Only during breeding season does the red-cockaded woodpecker have red stripes on its cap.

BYE, BYE, BLACKBIRD

In recent years some of Mississippi's most serious ecological problems have actually involved the overpopulation of certain animals. As in many parts of the country, people are concerned about the steadily increasing number of white-tailed deer that crowd the forests and sometimes wander into residential neighborhoods. But the most troubling and spectacular problems have involved the state's bird population.

In the late 1980s hundreds of thousands of blackbirds (above), cowbirds, and starlings began roosting each summer in a small patch of woods just outside of Tupelo, in the northeastern part of the state. The birds' chirping was so loud that it could be heard inside cars with closed windows speeding by on the Natchez Trace Parkway. And flying together, the birds occasionally darkened the noonday sky and actually prevented airplanes from landing at the local airport. After various failed efforts to frighten the birds away, the only way to disperse the birds was by cutting down several acres of trees outside Tupelo. Mysteriously the birds then abandoned the area, leaving the remainder of the region's dense forests undisturbed. As of 2007, they have not returned.

The red-cockaded woodpecker has become threatened by the rapid harvesting of pine trees in Mississippi and throughout the Southeast. Many of the birds' nests have been accidentally destroyed by woodcutters, and great numbers of birds have been driven from the area or have died. There are now fewer than ten thousand red-cockaded woodpeckers remaining in the entire Southeast, many of them scattered throughout the pine forests of southwestern Mississippi. Today scientists, federal and state agencies, and the local lumber industry are trying to preserve the sections of forest in which these rare birds live.

Of Mississippi's mammals the Louisiana black bear and the southeastern bat are the only endangered species at this time. However, the silver-haired bat, Indiana bat, and Florida panther have become extinct in Mississippi in spite of having been listed as endangered species for many years. Other animals that no longer make their homes in Mississippi are the tiger salamander, Bay Springs salamander, ivory-billed woodpecker, rock bass, western sand darter, pygmy killifish, sturgeon chub, flathead chub, western fanshell, Tombigbee moccasinshell, eastern indigo snake, Carey hawksbill, and southern hognose snake.

Most of these animals are no longer living in Mississippi because they lost their natural habitats. For many of them, home was in the wetlands. Little by little, Mississippi's wetlands have yielded to agriculture, housing, and industrial development. In recent years Mississippi's officials have been working with the federal government to stop the loss of these important lands. Wetlands not only provide homes for fish and other wildlife but also help control erosion and improve water quality.

CLIMATE

"Mississippi means hot. That's all there is to it," explains a motel manager in Meridian. "From June to September, you can pretty much count on things here being hot and humid and miserable. And you'd just as well get used to it—because there's not a thing you can do about it."

Mississippi is known for long summers, short winters, and high humidity throughout the year. Mississippi winters are typically mild. Even the lightest snowfall is rare, and the average low temperature is well above freezing—hovering around 38 degrees Fahrenheit for most of the season. Summers are usually hot, if not sweltering, especially in the southernmost part of the state. The thermometer frequently inches above the 100-degree mark during the long days of July and August.

Each summer all across the state, people do everything they can to fight the heat. Almost every home has an air conditioner. At outdoor occasions—like picnics, church socials, and sporting events—it is common to see entire crowds of people, especially older Mississippians, cooling themselves with handheld paper fans.

A great number of violent thunderstorms blow through the state each year. But even after its worst storms, Mississippi becomes a place of gentle beauty once again. "There's nothing like right after a big storm sets in," says a store owner from Philadelphia. "Leaves and limbs are scattered everywhere. Things get tossed every which way. But once it stops and the storm blows over, things get still and quiet. The air smells fresh and clear, and you see rainbows stretched across the road in front of you, sometimes two or three at a time."

The aftermath of a tornado or hurricane is not so peaceful. Tornadoes, with their funnel-shaped whirlwinds, cause terrible destruction when they touch down on land. In 1840 the second-most destructive tornado in U.S. history struck the city of Natchez in the southwestern part of the state, killing 317 people. Almost 100 years later, in 1936, another big twister demolished most of Tupelo, killing 216 people and seriously injuring 700 others. When it comes to having tornadoes classified as "strong" or "violent," Mississippi has been at the top of the list for the past several years. Between 1950 and 2005 Mississippi has averaged 26 tornadoes a year, with an average of 7 Mississippians killed by tornadoes each year. In 1953 Vicksburg lost 38 people to a tornado; in 1966, 57 people died in Jackson; in 1969, throughout Mississippi, 32 people died during a tornado. The Delta area lost 110 people in a tornado in 1971. In the late 1990s and early 2000s several tornadoes struck the state but claimed few lives.

Mississippi also experiences hurricanes—strong windstorms that develop over the ocean. If they reach land, their winds, which can blow faster than 260 miles per hour, and accompanying water cause great damage. The water can come in the form of rain or a storm surge, which is huge ocean waves that roll onto land. In August 1969 Hurricane Camille smashed into the Gulf Coast, killing 137 people. The storm caused heavy flooding and $510 million in property damage along the Gulf Coast and more than 100 miles inland. Some people estimate that Camille's winds exceeded 200 miles per hour! In fact, Camille's storm surge was strong enough to cut Ship Island in half. Now, there are two islands—East Ship Island and West Ship Island. The water between the islands is called Camille Cut.

On August 29, 2005, Hurricane Katrina, the worst natural disaster in U.S. history, hit the Gulf Coast and slowly moved across Mississippi on its way northeast. More than 80 miles of Mississippi's Gulf Coast were completely destroyed, and forty-nine of Mississippi's eighty-two

A fishing boat washed ashore during Hurricane Katrina in August 2005.

counties were declared disaster areas. Many Mississippians did not take the hurricane warnings seriously and therefore did not evacuate their homes. They thought that because they had survived Camille, they would also survive Katrina. At least 230 Mississippians lost their lives during Katrina. Those who survived the storm were left with more than 45 million cubic yards of debris—former homes, businesses, boats, and trees—to clean up. In all, 70,000 housing units were completely destroyed or severely damaged. Another 160,000 housing units were less severely damaged.

Chapter Two

A Rich and Troubled Past

All across the state, travelers encounter reminders of Mississippi's rich but troubled past. The great cotton plantations of the Delta recall the backbreaking servitude of the slaves and sharecroppers who cleared the land and harvested its crops. Parks and monuments throughout the state mark Civil War battle sites and memorialize the thousands of young men who died defending the Confederacy. Streets, high schools, and community centers in dozens of cities and towns proudly bear the names of slain civil rights leaders of the 1950s and 1960s. Even the state's musical legacy—the blues and gospel heard everywhere from barrooms to churches to concert halls—returns again and again to the injustice, violence, and finally the dramatic changes that have swept across the state during the past 150 years.

THE FIRST INHABITANTS

About 12,000 years ago the first people arrived in Mississippi. Most of them hunted and fished along the Mississippi River. Little is known about these

A statue in Vicksburg National Military Park honors those who fought in the Civil War.

earliest of Mississippi's settlers. The first people about whom much is known belonged to what is called the Mississippian Culture. They are also known as Mound Builders. By about 1,200 years ago they had built huge earthen structures at the centers of their villages. With the weathering that has taken place over the years, these structures now look like rounded mounds. Many mounds were used as burial grounds. On some mounds village leaders had their homes built. Deep postholes on other mounds lead archaeologists to think forts were built atop them. Mounds located near rivers might have been built as refuges in case of flooding.

Throughout Mississippi a few mounds still remain. Winterville Mounds State Park is located north of Greenville. Fifteen mounds stand there—one of them is about 55 feet tall. Nanih Waiya Mound, in the

One ancient mound in Mississippi is the Bear Creek Mound, built between 1200 and 1300 C.E. along the Natchez Trace.

northeastern corner of Neshoba County, rises about 35 feet and covers about 1 acre of ground. Emerald Mound, northeast of Natchez, is considered the second-largest mound in the United States. It stands about 35 feet high and covers 8 acres. Clay cups and bowls, peace pipes with carvings, and stone axes and spades are a few of the things archaeologists have found at Emerald Mound. The builders of the Nanih Waiya Mound are believed to be the ancestors of the Choctaw people, and Emerald Mound was probably built by the ancestors of the Natchez people.

NATIVE AMERICANS

By the 1500s about 30,000 Native Americans were living in what is now Mississippi. The largest groups were the Choctaw in the center of the state, the Chickasaw in the north, and the Natchez near present-day Natchez. Smaller groups included the Tunica and Yazoo along the Yazoo River and the Biloxi and Pascagoula along the Gulf Coast. Before the first European explorers or American settlers arrived, the region's Native Americans frequently exchanged crops, tools, and clothing. They had also established a 500-mile trade route between southwestern Mississippi and central Tennessee. Years later this trail would be used by white settlers and would come to be known as the Natchez Trace, connecting Natchez, Mississippi, to Nashville, Tennessee.

The Choctaw believed that the birthplace of their nation was at the Nanih Waiya Mound. They were a generally peaceful people but would fight when necessary. They lived in villages in thatch-roofed homes made of bark covered with mud. Skillful farmers, the Choctaw grew enough beans, corn, and pumpkins to trade with other groups. Choctaw men also hunted deer and bear; women and children gathered nuts and berries.

A Choctaw camp on the Mississippi River

The Chickasaw, whose headquarters were near present-day Tupelo, had a similar language to that of the Choctaw and shared other cultural characteristics with them. Known as fierce warriors, the Chickasaw learned the art of war at a young age, and war chiefs were highly respected. The Chickasaw also created extensive trade routes throughout the Southeast.

Like the Choctaw, the Natchez were successful farmers, growing beans, corn, and squash. They also hunted, fished, and gathered nuts and berries. The Natchez are best known for the large temples and chiefs' homes they built atop earthen pyramids. Ordinary people lived in square homes built out of sun-baked mud and straw and covered with arched cane roofs.

DE SOTO AND THE LOST CITY OF GOLD

Spaniard Hernando de Soto and his exploring party were the first Europeans to reach the area that is now Mississippi. De Soto landed in North America in 1539 and established himself as the colonial governor of Florida. Then, he embarked on a quest to find the lost "City of Gold" that he had heard described in Indian legends. The following year De Soto crossed into the area now known as Mississippi, probably near the current site of Columbus.

In Mississippi De Soto encountered a large encampment of Chicacas, who later became known as Chickasaws. At first the Indians received the Spaniards peacefully. But when De Soto enslaved several of them and forced them to carry supplies during the remainder of his journey, the Chickasaws fought back. One night they attacked the Spanish campsite, setting fire to wagons and huts while De Soto and his men slept. When the smoke cleared, forty of De Soto's men were dead, and his livestock and supplies were almost completely destroyed.

With little except the clothes on their backs, the Spaniards fled the smoldering remains of their camp and headed west, where De Soto still believed he would find the City of Gold. A few weeks later their march was halted by the vast waters of the Mississippi River. For De Soto the awe-inspiring river was just one more obstacle in his quest for gold. He put his men to work building rafts, and they crossed the Mississippi into what is now Arkansas.

Hernando de Soto greets Native Americans at the Mississippi River.

In 1542, after months of wandering lost through the swamps and forests of Arkansas, De Soto became ill and died suddenly. A year later the few surviving explorers rafted down the great river into the Gulf of Mexico, never having found the lost City of Gold.

SMOKING PIPES OF PEACE

Another 140 years would pass before Europeans again ventured into present-day Mississippi. In 1682 French explorer René-Robert Cavelier, Sieur de la Salle, entered the region. La Salle was much more skilled at befriending the native population than De Soto had been. He was also more respectful of the importance of the great river to the west. He recognized that the Mississippi River was destined to serve as an important waterway in the New World, and he wasted no time in claiming its shores for France.

René-Robert Cavelier, Sieur de la Salle claimed Mississippi for France in 1682.

The powerful Natchez tribe had several large settlements along the river. La Salle visited their villages, smoking peace pipes and exchanging gifts with their leaders. For the next thirty years the French enjoyed peaceful relations with the Natchez, and

France expanded its claims to include outposts on the Gulf Coast. In 1699 Pierre Le Moyne, sieur d'Iberville, established a colony in Biloxi.

The luck of the French quickly changed, in 1715, however, when the territorial governor Antoine de la Mothe, sieur de Cadillac, offended the inhabitants of one Natchez settlement by refusing to share a peace pipe with their chief. At this time Mississippi was part of the French territory known as Louisiana. The Indians expressed their anger by killing several of Cadillac's men, and many violent skirmishes followed between the French and the Natchez. In 1729 the French, under Jean-Baptiste Le Moyne, sieur de Bienville, finally defeated the Natchez, driving them from their homes to lands west of the Mississippi River. The few Natchez who remained on the eastern side of the river eventually joined neighboring Chickasaw villages.

Toward the end of the seventeenth century, France and England began arguing over the ownership of their settlements throughout the New World. For the next seventy-five years they fought a series of battles—known as the French and Indian Wars—over these disputed land claims. During the wars the British government returned Mississippi to its original Choctaw and Chickasaw inhabitants and declared it off-limits to all white settlers.

Even after the American colonists declared their independence and defeated the British in the Revolutionary War, the region that would become Mississippi remained sparsely occupied by white settlers for more than twenty years. Finally, with the formation of the Mississippi Territory in 1798, settlement increased.

Eventually white settlers began pouring into the area, and the Chickasaws and Choctaws were forced onto reservation lands in unsettled territories west of the Mississippi. By 1830 only a few remained in Mississippi. They are the ancestors of today's Choctaw people.

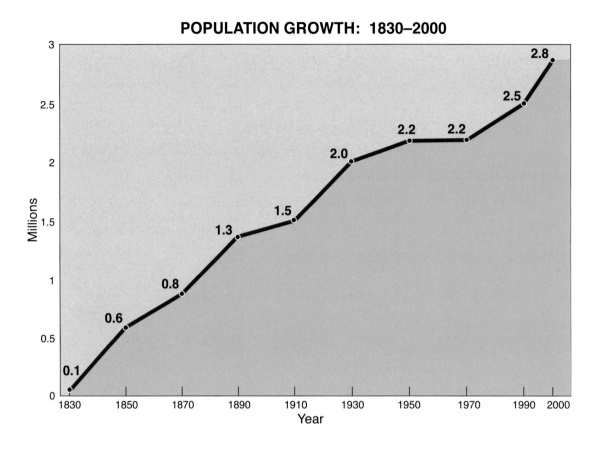

POPULATION GROWTH: 1830–2000

SLAVES ARRIVE IN THE DELTA

By 1817 Mississippi had finally attracted enough settlers for Congress to name it the nation's twentieth state. At the time very little of the state's land had actually been cleared for planting. When the first white settlers had arrived in the Delta, the land was an uncultivated jungle of forests and swamps.

However, the Mississippi River and the rich soil spreading out from its eastern banks were too important for the young nation's economy to remain undeveloped for long. In the 1830s wealthy developers from across the country began to purchase huge plots of land throughout the Delta.

Their goal was to grow cotton on the region's dark, fertile soil. The invention of the cotton gin by Eli Whitney in 1793 had made it easier to remove the cotton seeds from the fiber. This turned cotton into one of the nation's most profitable crops. Some records also show that a cotton gin was in operation in 1740 in Pascagoula.

Before the seeds could be planted and the cotton bolls could be harvested, however, the land had to be cleared of thickets and trees, and the region's vast swamps had to be drained. Between 1830 and 1860 thousands of African men, women, and children were brought to the Delta as slaves to perform these grueling tasks.

During the 1830s slaves endured hard labor in Mississippi's cotton fields.

In the 1500s, even before De Soto's expedition, the first Africans had arrived in what is now Mississippi as escaped slaves from Spanish colonies in the Caribbean. Most eventually became part of the Native American communities that De Soto and his men encountered. When Mississippi entered the Union, slaves made up about 40 percent of the state's overall population. By 1850, however, three out of four residents of Natchez were African-American slaves. By 1860 slaves would outnumber white settlers by as many as six to one in the Delta's richest counties.

On large plantations the slaves' hard, unpaid labor produced extraordinary wealth for their owners. These plantation owners used their newly acquired wealth to erect enormous homes, which they filled with expensive furniture and fine-art collections imported from Europe. In the old plantation system the owners' great mansions usually stood side by side with the slaves' simple living quarters.

Wealthy landowners reaped the benefits of their land's crops.

The cultivation of cotton in the Delta was brought to an abrupt halt by the outbreak of the Civil War on April 12, 1861. For several decades Northern and Southern leaders had been quarreling over the relationship between the state and federal governments. Many Northerners argued for a strong central government, which would develop and enforce the same set of rules for all states. Southerners favored a looser form of national government. Under their plan each individual state would have much more authority in establishing the rules and regulations by which it was governed. In the years before the war the issue of slavery became one of the central conflicts between the nation's Northern and Southern leaders.

On January 9, 1861, three months before the war began, Mississippi had followed South Carolina to become the second state to secede formally from the Union. The rebellious states soon formed the Confederate States of America. The new nation's first president, Jefferson Davis, was a Mississippian.

From the early days of the conflict, the Union commander Ulysses S. Grant knew that he had to capture the city of Vicksburg on the Mississippi River to win the war. Vicksburg is perched on bluffs high above a sharp bend in the river. Confederate cannons lined the bluffs, easily preventing Union riverboats from transporting goods and troops farther south. Grass-covered hills and ravines protected the city on all sides, making it virtually impossible to attack by land.

Jefferson Davis became president of the Confederate States of America in 1861.

After months of assaults Grant and his troops failed to capture the city. In May 1863 he decided to cut off the Confederates' supplies and starve them into surrender. This began the Siege of Vicksburg. The Confederate soldiers and townspeople of Vicksburg held out for almost two months—surviving largely on berries, mule meat, and sassafras tea—before they surrendered on July 4. After yet another two years of fighting, the Confederate general Robert E. Lee surrendered to Grant in Virginia. The North had won the Civil War.

The Union army took possession of Vicksburg on July 4, 1863.

RECONSTRUCTION

Mississippi was in shambles when the war ended. Raids by Union soldiers had destroyed roads and railroad lines. Factories and farms had gone up in smoke. At the time the war began, only 10 percent of the Delta had been cleared for planting. Large planters were now left with huge tracts of land to be cleared but without slave labor to do the work.

The situation was hardly better for the freed slaves. Despite their new legal rights, African Americans often found themselves with no place to stay and no source of income. In the years that followed the war, some freed slaves remained on their old plantations to work as hired hands for their former masters.

Over the next few decades a system known as sharecropping became increasingly common in Mississippi and throughout the South.

Through this arrangement laborers rented land, housing, seed, and supplies from landowners in exchange for half of the crops they raised. Workers hoped to earn enough money eventually to purchase the land outright, but this rarely happened. In fact, most sharecroppers sank deeper and deeper in debt to the landowners. In just a few years the majority of black farmers and poorer whites in Mississippi were trapped in this new form of economic slavery—permanently bound to their employers by enormous debts.

On rented land, sharecroppers hoped to grow and sell enough crops to eventually have the money to purchase their own land.

In the years immediately following the war, the period known as Reconstruction, the presence of the occupying Union army ensured that freed slaves enjoyed the rights and protections to which they were legally entitled. As the troops withdrew in 1876, however, the freedom of black Mississippians disappeared with them. Soon, blacks were prevented from voting and holding political office. By the end of the nineteenth century a formal system of segregation, known as the Jim Crow laws, had been put in place through the 1890 Mississippi state constitution. Blacks were excluded from many public places, including white schools and libraries. When black citizens were admitted to such places as theaters, ballparks, or public transportation, they were forced to sit or stand in special sections, usually in the back.

The Great Depression, which began in 1929 and lasted into the 1930s, was particularly hard on Mississippi. Early in the century a tiny insect called the boll weevil had first appeared in the state's cotton fields. During the Depression the boll weevil invaded the cotton fields by the millions. Entire crops were quickly destroyed, leaving both farm owners and fieldworkers with no way to support themselves. Faced with poor work conditions—and often the prospect of no work at all—thousands of Mississippians left the state and headed north to Chicago and other cities.

The Great Depression of the 1930s hurt many in Mississippi.

THE LEGEND OF CASEY JONES

Mississippi is known for its tall tales about the colorful characters who have lived and died there. One of the most colorful was the locomotive engineer Casey Jones. He liked to drive fast—very fast—along Mississippi's flat fields and marshes.

Jones was popular among the farmers and small-town folks who lived along his route. As he would roar past, they would wave to him from beside the tracks. At night, when they heard his trademark long, drawn-out whistle rise and then slowly die out, they would turn over in their beds and say, "There goes Casey Jones."

On April 30, 1900, Jones was driving a large, old train. As he and his assistant, Sim Webb, rounded a curve outside the tiny town of Vaughn, they saw an enormous freight train moving slowly along the side track a few hundred yards ahead. They knew they were going to crash. The two old wood-frame trains were far too wide to pass without smashing into one another. And with Jones gunning the old train at almost 60 miles per hour, he couldn't stop in time to avoid a collision. "Jump, Sim, and save yourself!" Jones yelled as he threw on the brakes. Sim did jump, but Jones stayed with the train, pulling at the whistle to warn the workers up ahead. According to local legend, he still had one hand on the whistle and the other on the brake when his broken body was pulled from the wreckage.

THE CIVIL RIGHTS MOVEMENT

The more than one million African-American Mississippians who remained in the state during the 1930s and 1940s continued to face violence and oppression. Things began to change dramatically, however, during the civil rights movement of the 1950s and 1960s. In 1955 a fourteen-year-old African-American boy named Emmett Till was dragged from his great-uncle's cabin and murdered by white racists. A few days earlier Till, who was visiting from Chicago, had supposedly whistled at a white woman on the street. The African-American press in Chicago heard about the murder, and it soon became headline news around the nation. Suddenly the harsh, violent condition of race relations in Mississippi was being discussed and debated by people everywhere. Two men were tried for the murder but were quickly acquitted.

In the following years thousands of Mississippians risked their lives and their livelihoods to bring about racial equality in their state. They participated in protests, sit-ins, and voter-registration drives. One of the key events in that struggle occurred on October 1, 1962, when James Meredith became the first African-American student to enroll at the University of Mississippi. "Ole Miss," as the university is called, was regarded by many people as the last stronghold of the white Mississippi ruling class.

In the following year, on June 12, 1963, Medgar Evers, a prominent civil rights activist, was shot in the back in his own driveway in Jackson by Byron De La Beckwith, a member of the White Citizens' Council. Beckwith bragged openly about committing that crime. However, in two separate trials, the all-white juries could not reach a verdict. The international news coverage surrounding the Evers assassination increased pressure for the passage of the Civil Rights Act of 1964, which banned segregation in Mississippi and throughout the nation.

James Meredith makes his way to class as the first African American at the University of Mississippi.

In 1994 Beckwith was tried a third time for his role in Evers's slaying. This time he was found guilty and sentenced to life in prison. Each day during the trial, newspaper headlines served as a painful reminder for adult Mississippians of one of the low moments in their state's history, and young Mississippians received a disturbing lesson about their past.

As painful as the experience was, the trial was also an act of healing for many Mississippians, as African Americans and whites came together to acknowledge a past injustice. "People want to act like bad things didn't happen, and I understand that. But you can't get past something till you admit it happened," explained an African-American restaurant owner in Clarksdale. "That trial was something we needed. Something all of us needed—not just black folks—to let us get on with our lives."

In the late 1990s and early 2000s Mississippi continued to right past wrongs done to the state's African Americans. In 2002 the state finally settled a lawsuit from 1975. The suit had claimed that the state-run predominantly black universities received less funding than those attended mainly by white students. As settlement the state agreed to grant $500 million to three black universities—Alcorn State, Jackson State, and Mississippi Valley State. In 2004 investigations reopened in the Emmett Till murder case to determine if others had been involved in his death. In 2007 a grand jury determined that the case should be closed because of a lack of evidence. In June 2006 city officials in McComb apologized to ten of its former residents. They had been high school students in 1961 when they were expelled for taking part in civil rights activities. Although they had finished high school elsewhere—many of them also going to college—they returned to McComb for a high school graduation ceremony held in their honor.

For many Mississippians August 29, 2005, will be a defining date in their lives. Everything before that date will be referred to as "Before Katrina"; everything after that, "After Katrina." Katrina, of course, was the hurricane that destroyed whole towns and caused billions of dollars in damage. Although Mississippians had lived through many hurricanes and tornadoes before that, Katrina was the worst natural disaster ever to hit anywhere in the United States. Entire towns were destroyed; huge casino barges were shoved ashore; boats and cars were tangled together on top of completely demolished homes. The governor immediately called out the state's National Guard units, to keep order and to help in recovery efforts. By early 2007 almost 100 percent of the debris had been cleared, many of the casinos and their hotels were back in

Hurricane Katrina devastated much of Mississippi, though Mississippians have been working hard to rebuild what was lost.

operation, traditional parades and festivals were being held, and new housing was going up. Stronger, safer buildings are being constructed to withstand hurricane winds and storm surges. However, complete recovery is going to take years. For all the damage Katrina did, it also pulled Mississippians closer together as they go about the business of rebuilding a large part of their state.

Chapter Three

Common Ground

Since the earliest days of statehood, Mississippi has been divided along racial lines—a distinction that continues to separate many of the state's people. Beneath the deep-seated racial divisions, however, African-American and white Mississippians are surprisingly united about a number of issues. The most important of these are their emphasis on friendliness and hospitality, their love of small-town life, and their common religious beliefs.

THE HOSPITALITY STATE

All across Mississippi, people take great pride in their state's reputation for friendliness and good manners. Mississippi has long been known as the Hospitality State, and Mississippians go out of their way to live up to the name.

From a tiny soul food café in the heart of the Delta to the sleek, fashionable shops of Jackson's Highland Village, visitors are always welcomed with the same friendly greeting. "How are *you*?" asks the speaker, her voice rising and stretching the last word into two long syllables. "Just *how* can I be of help to you?"

Though racially divided historically, all Mississippians are proud of their rich culture and heritage.

"It's just the way we are, I guess, the way we're taught to be," explained a sales clerk in Gulfport. "I was always taught to say 'Yes, sir,' and 'Yes, ma'am,' and to ask after people, even people I didn't know very well. Whenever I see somebody—either here at the store or the rest of the time—I just naturally want to know who they are and how they're doing. And I think that's the way most people are in Mississippi."

In fact, one of the first things many visitors to the state notice is that it is virtually impossible to go anywhere—or do anything—without somehow ending up in a conversation. Complete strangers can be seen chatting together in bookstores and coffee shops as if they were the oldest of friends. Even the simplest questions are often greeted with lengthy, drawn-out replies. Ask someone on a street corner for directions, and you may suddenly find yourself treated to a colorful history of your destination.

This hospitality is valued equally by African-American and white Mississippians. Many of the state's celebrated writers, such as Eudora Welty and William Faulkner, have demonstrated in their work how this friendliness and respect can bring people from different backgrounds together, especially in times of conflict and hardship.

Mississippi authors have also demonstrated the dark side of their state's seductive friendliness and charm. Writers as diverse as the late playwright Tennessee Williams and the contemporary novelist John Grisham have shown how polite words and friendly smiles can sometimes hide more troubling and complex feelings.

In most cases, however, the friendliness and civility are completely sincere and have a profound impact on the quality of life in Mississippi. Even in the state's large cities, visitors encounter a peaceful, small-town atmosphere that seems like a throwback to an earlier time.

THE ANGER BENEATH THE SURFACE

In the following passage from his autobiographical novel, *Black Boy*, Richard Wright describes how black Mississippians have frequently been forced to hide their ambitions and frustrations behind a protective veil of civility and good manners.

I began to marvel at how smoothly the black boys acted out the roles that the white race had mapped out for them. Most of them were not conscious of living a special, separate, stunted way of life. Yet I knew that in some period of their growing up—a period that they had no doubt forgotten—there had been developed in them a delicate, sensitive controlling mechanism that shut off their minds and emotions from all that the white race had said was taboo. Although they lived in an America where in theory there existed equality of opportunity, they knew unerringly what to aspire to and not to aspire to.

In small towns throughout the state, elderly men still sometimes greet one another in coat, hat, and tie at courthouse benches or along the town square. On the state's highways and back roads, farmers still look up from their machinery to wave at passing cars.

According to a young journalist in Oxford, this warmth and hospitality is what makes Mississippi so special to the people who live there. "I think what really sets Mississippi apart is the way people actually listen to each other," the young man explains. "Folks here really stop and take the time to hear what the other person is saying, even people who only know each other casually. To me, this gives Mississippi a certain closeness and intimacy that you don't find in other places, not even in other parts of the South."

There is a warmth and genuine friendliness among Mississippians.

HUSH PUPPIES

Hush puppies, one of Mississippi's most popular foods, are usually served as a side dish with catfish or other fried foods. During the Civil War, Confederate cooks invented these deep-fried balls of cornmeal as a meager main dish for starving soldiers. According to one story, the dish earned its name because military dogs, which were often even hungrier than their masters, would scamper to where the hush puppies were being prepared and yelp loudly until they were fed. "Hush, puppies!" the cooks supposedly yelled as they tossed the dogs hot morsels from the pan.

Have an adult help you prepare your own delicious, steaming-hot hush puppies.

Vegetable oil
1 cup white cornmeal
1/3 cup sugar
1 teaspoon salt
2 teaspoons baking powder
1 to 2 tablespoons onion, minced
2 cups water
6 tablespoons butter

Using a deep skillet, heat 2 inches of oil for 60 seconds. Combine cornmeal, sugar, salt, baking powder, and onion in a medium-sized bowl. Combine water and butter in a small saucepan and bring to a boil over high heat. Pour over dry ingredients, and stir rapidly to blend. When the mixture is cool enough to handle, form into twenty to thirty balls. Drop balls into hot oil a few at a time. Be careful not to crowd the pan. Deep-fry for 3 to 4 minutes, turning as often as needed, until they are golden brown on both sides. Remove hush puppies from oil and drain on paper towels. Hush puppies are best when served hot and in large quantities.

With a population of about 2,910,000, Mississippi ranks thirty-first among the fifty states in number of people. Mississippi is one of the few states that have more people living in rural areas (53 percent) than in urban areas (47 percent). This does not mean all those rural people live on farms. No, most of them live in small towns. That is how Mississippians get to know one another so well. Small-town life is valued highly in Mississippi. In fact, when people from other states move to Mississippi, they usually choose to settle in small towns. Starting in the 1990s, former Mississippians—both African Americans and whites—began moving back to their hometowns. Most of these people had retired from jobs in midwestern or northeastern cities and wanted to go back home. They had never stopped thinking of Mississippi as home!

Even after Hurricane Katrina had destroyed about 70,000 housing units—apartment buildings, condominiums, and houses—and damaged about 160,000 more, most of Mississippi's Gulf Coast residents decided to stay in their state. Some moved in with friends and relatives in other parts of the state. Others moved inland and rented or bought replacement homes. Many others stayed or returned to where their homes had been. These people are living in trailers—240-square-foot homes provided by the Federal Emergency Management Agency (FEMA). Along the Gulf Coast thousands of these trailers dot the landscape where neighborhoods once stood. "It's a tight squeeze for a family, but it's home for now," remarked one trailer dweller. By 2007 approximately 90,000 people were still living in FEMA trailers.

A displaced family makes a FEMA trailer their home in the wake of Hurricane Katrina.

ETHNIC MISSISSIPPI

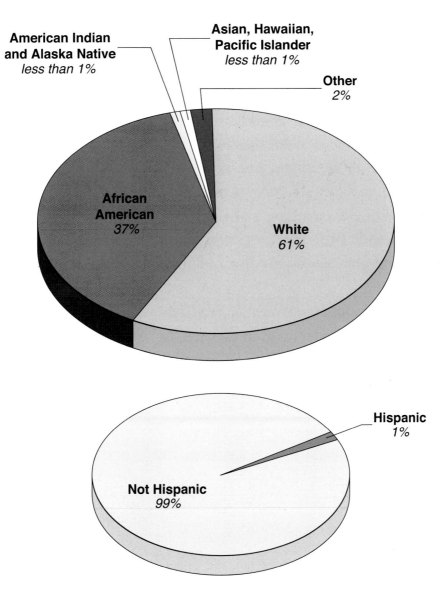

American Indian and Alaska Native
less than 1%

Asian, Hawaiian, Pacific Islander
less than 1%

Other
2%

African American
37%

White
61%

Hispanic
1%

Not Hispanic
99%

Note: A person of Cuban, Mexican, Puerto Rican, South or Central American, or other Spanish culture or origin, regardless of race, is defined as Hispanic.

If there is a single theme that unites and separates the people of Mississippi, it is the uneasy relationship between African-American and white Mississippians. Mississippi has the second-lowest percentage of white residents (61 percent) and the highest percentage of African-American residents (37 percent) in the fifty states. All told, about 98 percent of Mississippians are either African American or white; less than two out of one hundred belong to any other group—one of the smallest numbers of any state.

A half century ago the novelist William Faulkner described Mississippi's troubled history of race relations with these now-famous words: "The past is never dead. It's not even past." Today, Faulkner's words still ring true. All across Mississippi, African Americans and whites are still struggling to make sense of their state's painful history of injustice and racial conflict.

Mississippi's ethnic divisions rests mainly on its African-American and white residents.

Some of the most heated conflicts have concerned the state's symbols. An ongoing debate surrounds the continued use of the Confederate "stars and crossed bars" in the present-day Mississippi flag. Opponents of the current flag explain that it is impossible for them to look at it and not be reminded of the suffering of African-American Mississippians under slavery. The flag's supporters contend that the old Confederate symbol represents both the best and the worst aspects of their state's past—both the injustice and white supremacy of the past and the hospitality, civility, and honor in which Mississippians still take pride. "The whole thing is really confusing, and I don't see how we're ever going to resolve it to suit everybody," explains a student at Mississippi College, who supports keeping the old flag. "I agree that there are a lot of negative things about our flag—and the past history of our state, for that matter—but you can't just get rid of the flag. I mean, that's who we are, for better and for worse." In 2001 Mississippi's voters were given the choice between a newly designed flag and the old flag. They decided to keep the old one with the "stars and bars."

In the past few years many African-American students at the University of Mississippi in Oxford have complained about the singing of "Dixie," a nostalgic ballad about the joys of plantation life, and the waving of the Confederate flag at the school's football games. In 1997 the student senate banned all flags on poles at the games and discouraged students from bringing any Confederate flags into the stadium. "Dixie," however, is still heard occasionally.

Mississippians have chosen to keep the Confederate flag as a state symbol, even against opposition.

The university's longtime mascot, Colonel Rebel, also came under fire. The Colonel, a student dressed as an elderly, white-haired gentleman in a gray Confederate uniform, appeared at sporting events. For many students the Colonel was not an appropriate symbol for a university that welcomed students and faculty from other ethnic groups. As a result of those complaints, Colonel Rebel no longer is seen at University of Mississippi sporting events.

One step at a time, African-American and white Mississippians are finding resolutions to these controversies. However, the feelings among both groups are much too strong to allow an easy solution. What both African-American and white Mississippians do agree about, however, is that more and more people in both groups are now committed to working together and finding solutions to their problems.

"Medgar Evers and James Meredith both said that if we ever turn the corner on race, Mississippi will be the best place to live," says David Sansing, a historian at the University of Mississippi. "We have turned the corner," he says. But sometimes, he adds, it seems like Mississippians are just going in a circle. "Maybe we'll get off of it one day. But at least we're in motion, and that's more than you can say for much of the country."

Mississippi's smaller ethnic groups include Native Americans, Asians, and Hispanics. Native Americans make up only about 0.5 percent of Mississippi's population (14,605 people). Most of them are members of the Mississippi band of Choctaws, descendants of the people who refused to leave Mississippi in the 1830s. They live on their ancestors' lands in Neshoba County, on or near the Choctaw Reservation.

In the 1970s the Choctaws faced widespread unemployment; fewer than one in four adults was able to find a job, either on or off the reservation. In 1979 the tribal council began planning the development of an

80-acre industrial park, which they hoped would reverse the chronic poverty and unemployment among their people. In the past twenty years the Choctaw government has developed many new businesses throughout the reservation's industrial park. The reservation has become the area's largest employer as owner and operator of the Pearl River Resort, which has two casinos, two golf courses, and a huge water park. Besides the casino the reservation also has arrangements to make parts for the Ford Motor Company. Now more than 85 percent of the adult Choctaw population has full-time employment. Although the Choctaws are part of modern life, they also treasure their traditional culture and continue to pass down their native language to their children.

In 2002 Chief Philip Martin (right) of the Choctaws celebrated the construction of the Pearl River Resorts Golden Moon Hotel and Casino.

THE GREEN CORN FESTIVAL

Each July the Mississippi Choctaws hold the Choctaw Indian Fair at their reservation in Neshoba County. The festival is modeled after the ancient Green Corn Festival, the most sacred day of the year for the Choctaw people. Besides drawing crowds of locals and tourists, the festival also serves as a time of reunion for the Choctaws.

Participants in the original Green Corn Festival spent three to four days dancing and chanting to celebrate the harvest of their most important crop. Today participants dress in colorful traditional costumes to re-create the harvest dance and other traditional dances and social activities. Among the highlights are the animal dances, in which the Choctaws dance in costumes representing ducks, quails, snakes, and raccoons, and an annual stickball tournament.

Another 0.7 percent of Mississippi's population (20,000 people) traces its ancestry to Asia. Since the early 1900s Chinese people have lived in the state. Many of them settled in towns in the Delta region. Since the 1970s, at the end of the Vietnam War, Vietnamese families immigrated to Gulf Coast towns and cities. They found jobs in the seafood industry, working on shrimp boats or in food processing.

The largest of Mississippi's smaller ethnic groups is made up of Hispanics—about 1.7 percent (more than 49,000 people). During the 1990s many of them came from Mexico, while others emigrated from Honduras and Nicaragua. This was especially true after Hurricane Mitch destroyed their homes in Central America in 1998. Most of Mississippi's Hispanics live in Jackson, Biloxi, and Gulfport and make their livings building casinos or working in forestry industries. In recent years catfish-processing plants in the Delta have attracted great numbers of Hispanics. After Hurricane Katrina blew through Mississippi, many more Hispanics arrived to take construction jobs in the rebuilding of the Gulf Coast.

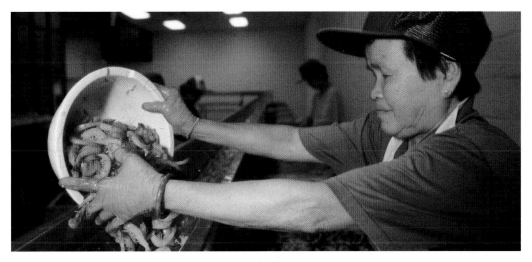

Many Asians in Mississippi earn their living in the seafood industry.

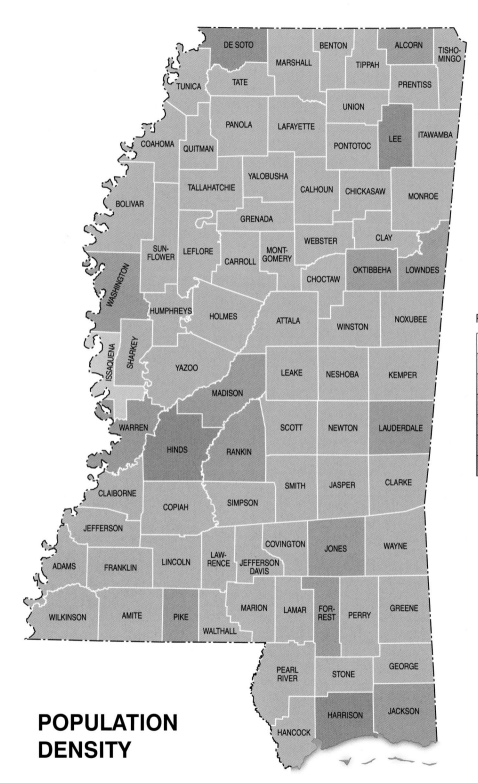

POPULATION DENSITY

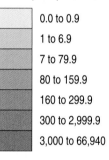

Persons per square mile

	0.0 to 0.9
	1 to 6.9
	7 to 79.9
	80 to 159.9
	160 to 299.9
	300 to 2,999.9
	3,000 to 66,940

Religion plays an important part in the lives of most Mississippians. Located near the buckle of the Bible Belt, Mississippi has more churches per capita than any other state. Crowded together at the center of the state's towns, the tall steeples of houses of worship seem to compete for the most prominent spot on the horizon. More modest churches, with green, well-shaded cemeteries in the back, are a frequent sight at major crossroads and on the outskirts of farm communities. Tiny, one-room churches can also be found at the narrow entrances to backcountry roads or on deeply rutted dirt roads, often shaded by a single tree.

Churchgoers leave their one-room church after services.

Christianity is the dominant religion in Mississippi. Almost 95 percent of the state's residents identify themselves as Christian, the third-highest percentage of any state. Sunday mornings are a major social event, as families around the state attend worship and then share a meal together at a favorite restaurant. "I always used to look forward to Sundays and church," recalls a former Mississippi resident who now lives in the Northeast. "It was the time when everyone came together—people whom you wouldn't normally see or who didn't socialize during the rest of the week. Sundays in Mississippi are the one time when everything and everyone comes together."

Almost half of all Mississippians are Southern Baptists, by far the state's most powerful and vocal denomination. Southern Baptists have had an enormous impact on the state's social and cultural life. They have funded the development of major colleges and hospitals throughout the state and have taken a leading, usually conservative, role in addressing important social issues. Methodists and Presbyterians are also well represented in Mississippi, particularly among white communities.

African Americans belong to a wide variety of denominations, including Pentecostal Holiness, African Methodist Episcopal, and a number of independent Baptist fellowships. The music and preaching that can still be heard at the services of these small, emotionally charged congregations has had an enormous impact on the culture of both Mississippi and the entire nation.

Although most Mississippians are Protestant, especially Baptist and Methodist, some Mississippians are Catholic, Jewish, or Muslim. Most of their houses of worship are located in the state's cities. For example, Clarksdale, Greenville, Meridian, and Jackson have Jewish synagogues. Gulf Coast cities, where French Catholics originally settled, have many Catholic churches. Each year at the beginning of the shrimping season, Catholic clergy bless the shrimp boats off the shores of Biloxi in the Blessing of the Fleet.

Baptist choir members perform during a church service.

Mississippi's Muslim community is small but growing. It includes black and white converts as well as Arabs and others who have immigrated to Mississippi. About four thousand Muslims live in Jackson and pray in mosques there.

A RICH MUSICAL TRADITION

From blues to gospel, from rock to pop, Mississippians love good music. During the late 1800s the music known as the blues was created on Mississippi's Delta plantations. Blues was the music of African-American fieldworkers and sharecroppers—the sons and daughters of freed slaves. They combined African rhythms and the call-and-response style of fieldworkers' songs with dark, brooding singing. Blues lyrics told the painful story of what it was like to be a poor black person living in a world ruled by wealthy whites.

VICKSBURG BLUES

The blues is one of the great contributions made by African Americans to American and world culture. The cotton fields and levees of Mississippi have been among the most fertile areas for the growth of the blues.

I've got those Vicksburg blues, and I'm singin' it everywhere I please.
I've got those Vicksburg blues, and I'm singin' it everywhere I please
Now, the reason I'm singin', it is to give my poor heart ease.

Now, I don't like this place, mamma, and I never will.
Now, I don't like this place, mamma, and I never will.
I can sit right here in jail and look at Vicksburg on the hill.

Among the many blues musicians born and raised in Mississippi are such legends as Charley Patton, John Lee Hooker, and Robert Johnson. Robert Johnson was probably the most influential early blues artist to claim Mississippi as his home. He was certainly the most mysterious. Born in 1911 in Hazlehurst, in southern Mississippi, he moved to the Delta town of Robinsonville when he was nine. As a teen Johnson showed little promise as a blues guitarist. Then he left town for a few months. When he returned, he could play and sing the blues in a way no one had heard before. A story started that Johnson had sold his soul to the devil in exchange for his newly acquired talent. Whatever happened, Johnson had only a few years to play his haunting blues music. He died when he was only twenty-seven years old.

Many blues musicians are known by their colorful nicknames, such as Ellas "Bo Diddley" Bates, McKinley "Muddy Waters" Morganfield, Chester "Howlin' Wolf" Burnett, and Riley B. King—"B. B. King." Currently B. B. King is hailed as the King of the Blues. Some of his well-known songs are "The Thrill Is Gone," "When Love Comes to Town," and "You Know I Love You." Every year at least fifty blues festivals take place throughout the state, although most of them are in Delta towns.

During the late 1800s and early 1900s African-American worshippers throughout Mississippi mixed elements of Methodist hymn singing, white evangelical preaching, and African chanting and drumming to create a new form of music. Known today as gospel, this music combines the dark, mournful quality of the blues with the joyful exuberance of traditional Christian hymns. The powerful, sometimes frenzied sermons of Baptist and Pentecostal preachers have also influenced the performing styles of rock-and-roll and rhythm-and-blues musicians.

B. B. King (right) and Bo Didley are two of the most well-known blues musicians from Mississippi.

Mississippi was also home to the man known as the Father of Country Music. Meridian resident Jimmie Rodgers worked for years as a brakeman for the railroads before he achieved fame as a country blues singer in the 1920s and 1930s, with such songs as "In the Jailhouse Now," "Frankie and Johnnie," and "Mule Skinner Blues." Rodgers had a distinctive, unforgettable singing style, ending the verses to many of his songs with a high-pitched yodel. When he died of tuberculosis in 1933, he was one of the nation's most popular recording artists, having sold more than twenty million records in the six years since his first single was released.

Elvis Presley, the king of rock and roll, was born in Mississippi.

Other Mississippians who have followed in Rodgers's country-music footsteps include Faith Hill, Charley Pride, LeAnn Rimes, Conway Twitty, and Tammy Wynette.

The king of rock and roll was also from Mississippi. Elvis Presley was born in a small white house in Tupelo on January 8, 1935. As a child Elvis was fascinated by the different kinds of music he heard around him—country music on the radio; the slow hymns he heard in church; the more explosive gospel songs he heard through the thin walls of African-American churches; and the dark, mournful blues songs played by the old African-American men on Main Street. Then Elvis heard a new form of music called rock and roll, which combined all the musical forms he enjoyed. Elvis cut his first song, "That's All Right (Mama)," when he was only nineteen years old, and the rest is history. By 1956 Elvis had become the biggest-selling recording artist in the history of American music, with hits such as the number-one pop single ("I Want You, I Need You, I Love You"), the number-one rhythm-and-blues single ("Heartbreak Hotel"), and the number-one country single ("I Forgot To Remember To Forget") ever. Two years later Elvis had sold more than 16 million records, including such classics as "Hound Dog," "Don't Be Cruel," and "Jailhouse Rock." Although Elvis won many awards, he was proudest of the ones he received for his gospel music. Like so many of Mississippi's musicians, Elvis also died young—at the age of forty-two. Other current Mississippians known for rock and pop music include Mac McAnally, Lance Bass of *NSYNC, Jimmy Buffett, Brandy Norwood, and the members of Blind Melon and 3 Doors Down.

Mississippians share deeply held religious beliefs, a commitment to hospitality, a fondness for small-town life, and a love of music. Together these factors give the state a way of life in which all Mississippians can take pride.

Chapter Four

Making and Breaking Laws

Each state has its own form of government and its own style of making, enforcing, and changing the laws by which it is governed. Throughout much of its history, Mississippi has balanced a conservative, slow-moving form of government with a radical, often violent tradition of protest and social dissent.

INSIDE GOVERNMENT

Mississippi is governed under a state constitution that was adopted in 1890. Since then there have been many amendments (changes). However, Mississippi's government, like those of the other states and the federal government, is divided into three branches: executive, legislative, and judicial.

Executive

Mississippi's chief executive is the governor, who is elected to a four-year term. The governor is responsible for preparing the state budget and

Built to house all of the branches of Mississippi's government, the capitol houses only the legislative and executive branches of government.

developing policies in areas such as education, law enforcement, and economic development. The governor also decides whether to sign or veto (reject) bills that the state legislature has approved.

Mississippi has traditionally had one of the weakest executive branches in the United States. This is partly because up until 1988, the governor was forbidden by the state constitution to serve consecutive terms. However, the governor could be elected more than once if there was a gap between the two terms. Since 1988 Mississippi's governors have been allowed to serve consecutive terms, but they can only be elected twice. This has given Mississippi's governors a stronger leadership role. For example, after Hurricane Katrina struck, Governor Haley Barbour, elected in 2004, immediately set up a special commission to devise strategies to rebuild the towns that had been destroyed.

The other officers in the executive branch are also elected to four-year terms and may serve any number of them. However, the lieutenant governor may not serve more than two terms in a row. Other elected executive officials are the secretary of state, treasurer, auditor, and attorney general. In Mississippi the commissioners of agriculture and commerce, public service and transportation, and insurance are also elected officials.

Mississippi governor Haley Barbour speaks to emergency management workers at their 2006 conference.

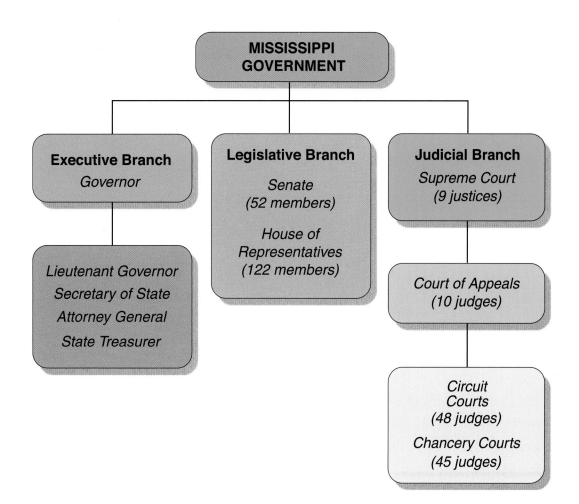

MISSISSIPPI GOVERNMENT

Executive Branch
Governor

Lieutenant Governor
Secretary of State
Attorney General
State Treasurer

Legislative Branch

Senate
(52 members)

House of
Representatives
(122 members)

Judicial Branch
Supreme Court
(9 justices)

Court of Appeals
(10 judges)

Circuit
Courts
(48 judges)

Chancery Courts
(45 judges)

Legislative

The Mississippi legislature is divided into a senate with 52 members and a house of representatives with 122 members. All state legislators are elected to four-year terms. The Mississippi state legislature has enormous powers, including drafting and passing laws and public policy, approving budgets, raising state revenues, and overseeing the state's administrative network. If enough legislators agree, the legislature can also overturn the governor's veto of a bill so that the bill becomes law anyway.

Judicial

The state's highest court, the supreme court, consists of nine judges who are elected to eight-year terms. The state's next-highest court is the court of appeals, consisting of ten judges who are elected to four-year terms. Mississippi has two types of trial courts: circuit courts, which hear both civil and criminal cases, and chancery courts, which try only civil cases.

When someone challenges a decision in one of the state's criminal courts, the case is heard by the court of appeals, which decides whether to uphold or overturn the lower court's decision. If the court of appeals' decision is also challenged, the matter is sent to the state supreme court for a hearing.

POLITICAL PARTIES

Mississippi has shifted in the past thirty years from one of the nation's most Democratic states to a powerful Republican stronghold. From Reconstruction to the mid-twentieth century, Mississippi was commonly regarded as the center of the Solid South of the Democratic Party. Between 1876 and 1944 Mississippians voted for the Democratic candidate in every major local, state, and national election.

Following World War II the legal rights of African Americans became an increasingly important issue in national politics. In greater and greater numbers, white voters in Mississippi began to turn their backs on liberal Democratic candidates who openly favored desegregation and racial equality. After the passage of the Voting Rights Act of 1965, more and more African Americans registered to vote, usually as members of the Democratic Party.

Since the mid-1970s Mississippi has become more Republican. In 1992 Kirk Fordice became the first Republican governor of the state since 1876.

An African-American man registers to vote at the Panola County Courthouse in 1966.

In 1978 Thad Cochran was elected as the state's first Republican senator since Reconstruction. He was joined in the U.S. Senate in 1989 by fellow Republican Trent Lott. From 1996 to 2001 Lott served as the majority leader of the U.S. Senate. He then served as the minority leader from 2001 to 2002. In 2006 he was elected to be the Republican Senate minority whip.

A DISSENTING PEOPLE

From the secretive activities of the racist Ku Klux Klan to the defiant public demonstrations of civil rights activists during the 1950s and 1960s, Mississippians have a long history of taking the law into their own hands.

In 1954 the U.S. Supreme Court declared the racial segregation of public schools to be unconstitutional. Calling this ruling "an illegal, immoral and sinful doctrine," Senator James O. "Big Jim" Eastland advised his fellow Mississippians not to obey it. "Southern people will not be violating the Constitution or the law," reasoned the senator, "when they defy this monstrous decision."

Almost a decade later state leaders were still openly defiant of the Supreme Court's ruling and the power of the federal government to enforce it. In 1962 Governor Ross Barnett attracted international attention over his dispute with U.S. attorney general Robert F. Kennedy concerning the admission of James Meredith as a student at the University of Mississippi. "A segregated Mississippi, now and forever," Barnett proclaimed to a stadium full of defiant white Mississippians just hours before giving in to the attorney general's demands.

Historically, black civil rights activists in the state have been even more defiant than their white, conservative counterparts in challenging laws with which they disagreed. During the 1950s and 1960s hundreds of African-American Mississippians were thrown into jail for taking part in unauthorized demonstrations or for refusing to obey laws that segregated citizens according to their race.

One of the bravest and most persistent of these people was Fannie Lou Hamer of Montgomery County. Hamer spent much of the 1960s organizing protests, encouraging African-American citizens to vote, and teaching them to read and write. She was harassed and arrested for her efforts, once enduring a brutal beating at the Montgomery County Jail in Winona.

In 1964 Hamer took her fight for freedom to the Democratic National Convention, introducing the nation to the proud belligerence of Mississippi activism. Angered that the state's Democratic Party had failed to

Fannie Lou Hamer was a cofounder of the Mississippi Freedom Democratic Party.

include African Americans in its delegation, Hamer led her own group of delegates into the convention hall. Officials refused to recognize Hamer's "Mississippi Freedom Democratic Party" representatives. But she and her fellow delegates refused to leave, even when they were threatened with arrest.

The Democratic National Committee offered Hamer two temporary seats and promised full representation for African-American Mississippi Democrats in the future, but she rejected the compromise. "We didn't come all this way for no two seats when all of us is tired," she explained in a televised interview heard around the world.

Though Hamer's group was never seated, she did force convention officials to admit that the old policy for selecting state delegates was unfair. By the end of the convention, people everywhere knew a lot more about the racial inequities of both Mississippi politics and the national Democratic Party. Since then, African-American Mississippi Democrats have always been fairly represented at conventions.

Despite Mississippi's many conflicts and hardships over the years, its citizens remain proud and determined. Today both African-American and white Mississippians speak enthusiastically about the political and economic developments made in their state during the past few years. And increasingly, members of both groups share a commitment to continue rethinking and rebuilding their state. "You have to admit," insists a teacher in McComb, "we have come a long, long way together. While the rest of the country was talking about the really tough issues—like desegregation and restructuring the economy—we were down here meeting them face to face. A lot of it may have been forced on us at the time, and some of us may have come through it kicking and scratching, but we came through it just the same, and we're better people for it now. I think pretty much everyone realizes that."

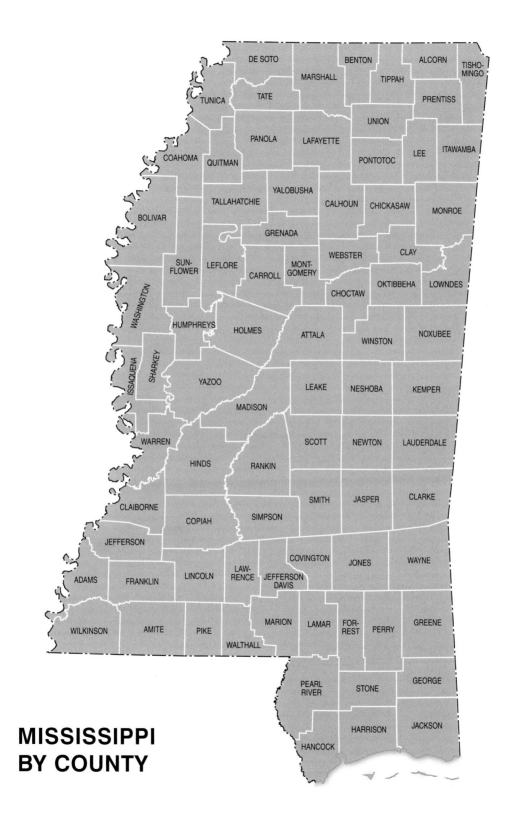

**MISSISSIPPI
BY COUNTY**

Former U.S. secretary of education Rod Paige speaks to Mississippi students about community leadership and education.

EDUCATION

Illiteracy and poor education have traditionally been enormous problems for Mississippi. As of 2006 roughly three-fourths of the state's adults are high school graduates, the lowest percentage in the nation. Only 17 percent of all adults have college degrees. In the early 2000s only 59 percent of high school students actually graduated. With limited classroom resources and salaries below the national average, teachers in the state face an uphill battle. Some progress is being made however. By the school year 2006–2007, teachers had received an almost 30 percent increase in salary over four years, and the amount spent per student by the government had increased by about 22 percent.

In spite of its long history of problems with education, Mississippi has an impressive set of colleges. Mississippi College, the state's oldest institution of higher learning, was founded in Clinton in 1826. The state also boasts three major state universities. The University of Mississippi, in Oxford, is the home of the Center for the Study of Southern Culture, one of the leading folk history archives in the country. Mississippi State University in Starkville has one of the premier agricultural research facilities in the Southeast. The University of Southern Mississippi, in Hattiesburg, is the state's youngest major university and the publisher of *The Mississippi Review*, which has featured works by some of America's most gifted contemporary writers.

Chapter Five

Cotton, Catfish, Casinos, and Construction

Mississippi has a diverse economy composed of agriculture, fishing, mining, manufacturing, and service industries. In spite of this diversity, Mississippi's economy lags behind that of most other states. At 7 to 7.5 percent, it has one of the country's highest unemployment rates. Mississippi also has the country's highest poverty rate, at more than 18 percent. The average household income is the third lowest in the United States. Many of Mississippi's economic problems can be traced to educational problems, such as the low percentage of high school graduates. In some areas jobs are available, but the available workers do not have adequate job skills. Many jobs are also directly or indirectly based on agriculture, such as farmwork and food processing. These types of jobs often pay low wages.

Finding a job in Mississippi is not easy. The state has one of the country's highest unemployment rates.

AGRICULTURE, FISHING, AND MINING

Most people find it hard to think about Mississippi without thinking of cotton. Up to the 1930s a majority of the state's citizens made their living either as cotton farmers or as fieldworkers, or in some other part of the textile industry. All this began to change when the boll weevil destroyed thousands of acres of unharvested cotton around the state. It suddenly became clear to many farmers that it was too risky to base the state's entire economy on a single crop. During the next few years, large tracts of cotton fields throughout Mississippi were planted with peas, soybeans, corn, and grains. At the same time the Balance Agriculture with Industry program was introduced to encourage the development of new businesses and the creation of new jobs in the state.

As a result of these changes, Mississippi farming is no longer the powerful economic force it once was. Today profits from farming provide only 3 percent of the state's gross annual product, and farming employs about 5 percent of the state's workers. Although the large cotton plantations of the Delta no longer dominate the state's economy, farming and farm life are still an important part of the state's appearance and personality. More than 42,000 active farms cover about one-third of the state. The average farm's size is 260 acres, and most of Mississippi's farms are family-owned and operated.

Some farmers in Mississippi raise hybrid corn.

The biggest agricultural moneymakers are livestock and livestock products, such as broiler chickens, eggs, cattle, sheep, and hogs. They make up more than half of Mississippi's farm economy. The leading crops are cotton, soybeans, rice, corn, and hay. Even with the dramatic reduction in cotton farming in the state, Mississippi still ranks as one of the nation's largest cotton producers. Other important crops include sweet potatoes, peas, beans, peaches, watermelons, and pecans.

The most significant development in the state's farm economy in recent years has been the introduction of catfish farming. In the Delta hundreds of abandoned plantation fields have been converted into fish hatcheries. Mississippi now has about four hundred catfish farms covering about

Beef production in Mississippi contributes more than $216 million toward the state's agricultural sector.

101,000 water-filled acres. The state has become the nation's leading producer of commercial catfish, with thousands of the fish shipped each day to restaurants and supermarkets around the country.

Commercial fishing takes place along Mississippi's Gulf Coast. Biloxi has a large fleet of shrimp boats. Other important catches from Gulf waters include crab, oysters, menhaden, red snapper, and a variety of sea trout. After Hurricane Katrina the first few fishing seasons were shortened, and the catches were limited to give the fish a chance to repopulate the waters.

Oil and natural gas extraction make up the bulk of Mississippi's mining industry. These mining products are found in the southern part of the state. In 2006 the city of Laurel had eighty-three working wells within the city limits. Other important mining products include clays, crushed limestone, sand, and gravel.

Oysters are farmed off the Biloxi coast.

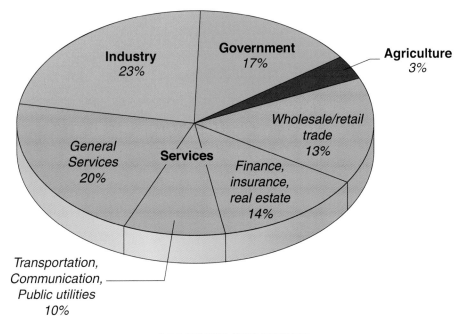

2005 GROSS STATE PRODUCT: $81 Billion

Industry
23%

Government
17%

Agriculture
3%

Wholesale/retail
trade
13%

General
Services
20%

Services

Finance,
insurance,
real estate
14%

Transportation,
Communication,
Public utilities
10%

MANUFACTURING

During the late 1900s and early 2000s industry has become a larger part of Mississippi's economy. Today manufacturing provides more than one-quarter of the state's annual income. One of Mississippi's largest industries is shipbuilding. A number of shipyards line the Gulf Coast, including Northrop Grumman Ship Systems' Ingalls Operations in Pascagoula, the state's largest private employer, with about 11,000 workers. Northrop Grumman builds ships for the U.S. navy and for cruise lines, as well as rigs for off-shore oil drilling. Ingalls suffered little damage from Hurricane Katrina.

Another growth industry is forestry and wood products. With more than half of its land covered by forests, Mississippi has traditionally been a leader in harvesting pine and hardwoods. Heavily loaded logging trucks have long been a familiar sight on freeways across the state.

Many small towns in the pinelands of the state's southeast corner rely heavily on paper mills for employment. In the past, most Mississippi lumber was shipped out of state for manufacturing. This has changed in recent years, however, with wood-processing factories opening up in such cities as Jackson, Columbus, and Natchez. Tupelo, in the state's northeast corner, has become one of the nation's major producers of hardwood furniture, which is now Mississippi's third-leading manufactured good.

Processed foods are the state's leading manufactured product. Catfish processing in the Delta, shrimp packaging in Biloxi and Pascagoula, and poultry processing in Laurel and Forest are among the leading processed-food products. Furniture making ranks second.

"MAKE MINE MISSISSIPPI"

In 1999 the Mississippi Development Authority began the "Make Mine Mississippi" program. It is a way for Mississippi businesses to let Mississippians and people in other states know that a product was made in Mississippi. Each product must be at least 51 percent produced, processed, or manufactured in Mississippi. Members receive the "Make Mine Mississippi" logo and up to $2,000 in government funding each year. They use the money for advertising or renting booths at trade fairs. Within five years, more than eight hundred businesses had joined the program—from catfish producers to pottery makers to specialty food makers. Jams, jellies, sweet potato treats, and praline candies made with Mississippi pecans are especially popular.

A worker at a catfish-processing plant oversees fillets on a conveyor belt.

Chemicals used for agriculture and industry are the state's third most important manufactured products. Transportation equipment is another important manufactured product. This includes cars and trucks built at the Nissan plant in Canton. Electrical parts for vehicles are produced in factories near Jackson.

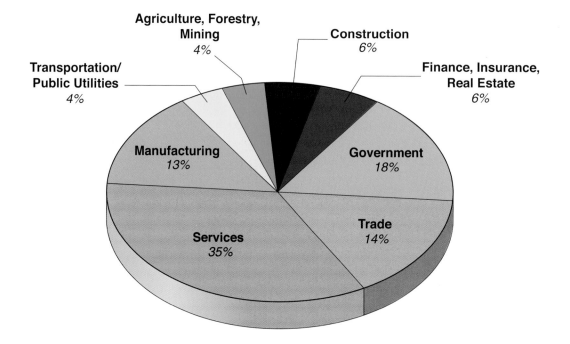

MISSISSIPPI WORKFORCE

Agriculture, Forestry, Mining
4%

Construction
6%

Transportation/
Public Utilities
4%

Finance, Insurance,
Real Estate
6%

Manufacturing
13%

Government
18%

Services
35%

Trade
14%

SERVICE INDUSTRIES

Trade and transportation, construction, government, and tourism are Mississippi's leading service industries. Mississippi trades with other states and more than one hundred countries every year. Canada and Mexico have long been the state's leading trade partners. In recent years Mississippi has developed strong trade relations with Saudi Arabia, the United Arab Emirates, and China. In 2005, $4 billion of Mississippi-made products were exported to countries around the world. Mississippi's trade flourishes because it has a strong transportation and shipping system. River barges carry goods to and from Vicksburg and Natchez—two major port cities on the Mississippi River. Ships from other countries can dock at the state's two deepwater ports in Pascagoula and Gulfport.

A tugboat pushes barges loaded with cargo on the Mississippi River.

EARNING A LIVING

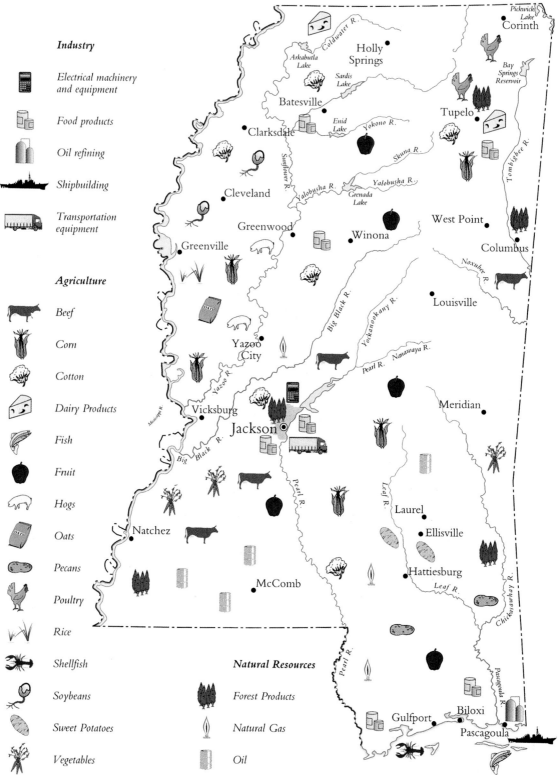

Industry

- Electrical machinery and equipment
- Food products
- Oil refining
- Shipbuilding
- Transportation equipment

Agriculture

- Beef
- Corn
- Cotton
- Dairy Products
- Fish
- Fruit
- Hogs
- Oats
- Pecans
- Poultry
- Rice
- Shellfish
- Soybeans
- Sweet Potatoes
- Vegetables

Natural Resources

- Forest Products
- Natural Gas
- Oil

Corinth
Pickwick Lake
Holly Springs
Arkabutla Lake
Sardis Lake
Batesville
Tupelo
Bay Springs Reservoir
Coldwater R.
Enid Lake
Clarksdale
Yokono R.
Skuna R.
Tombigbee R.
Cleveland
Yalobusha R.
Yalobusha R.
Grenada Lake
Sunflower R.
Greenwood
Winona
West Point
Columbus
Greenville
Noxubee R.
Louisville
Big Black R.
Yockanookany R.
Pearl R.
Nanawaya R.
Yazoo City
Yazoo R.
Meridian
Mississippi R.
Vicksburg
Jackson
Leaf R.
Laurel
Ellisville
Big Black R.
Pearl R.
Hattiesburg
Natchez
Leaf R.
McComb
Chickasawhay R.
Pascagoula R.
Gulfport
Biloxi
Pascagoula

In the 1990s construction boomed across the state as casinos, hotels, and other businesses went up along the Mississippi River and Gulf Coast. The destruction caused by Hurricane Katrina in 2005 necessitated a new round of construction. "Building Back Better Than Ever" became the slogan for this new construction. Architects and engineers developed plans for homes and other buildings that would withstand hurricane winds and water better. About 6 percent of the state's labor force works in construction. However, more workers are needed in this field.

The Mississippi State government and the U.S. government employ about 19 percent of Mississippi's workers. They work in Mississippi's state parks and in various national parks and national forests. Keesler Air Force Base in Biloxi and Columbus Air Force Base have a great number of both military and civilian employees. There is also a Sea Bee Base in Gulfport.

Tourism has also become a growing industry in Mississippi. Each year the state earns more than $5 billion from tourism. Much of the growth has come about since the 1990s when the state legislature first allowed casino gambling. About thirty large gambling casinos with accompanying hotels now stand in the Delta, in Tunica and Greenville; along the Mississippi River, in Vicksburg and Natchez; and along the Gulf Coast, in Bay St. Louis, Biloxi, and Gulfport. Thousands of visitors from other southern states and from the Midwest spend time and millions of dollars at the casinos. Other favorite tourist destinations are the pre–Civil War homes in Natchez, Vicksburg National Military Park, and the Gulf Coast's white, sandy beaches.

Chapter Six

Cities and Small Towns

Mississippi is a small but beautiful state—two characteristics in which its residents take particular pride. "We're a modest little state, and we're proud about that," beams a farmer from Greenville. "You don't have to travel far to see things here, and there's plenty of beautiful things to see wherever you go. Unlike other places these days, we're not overrun with big cities and tall buildings and lots and lots of people. The beauty of Mississippi is still peaceful and undisturbed, and I really do hope we can keep it that way."

Mississippi is primarily a rural state. On the state's highways, motorists spend most of their time observing forests and farmland. For those who follow the occasional signs leading off the highways, however, the state offers a surprising number of landmarks and historic sites.

THE NORTH

Tupelo, in Mississippi's northeastern hill country, is known primarily as the birthplace of the rock-and-roll pioneer Elvis Presley. The two-room house where Presley was born is located on a quiet, tree-lined street on the outskirts

Natchez, Mississippi, named after the Native-American tribe that once lived there, is one of the oldest cities in North America.

of town. On the hill behind the house sits a tiny chapel, along with a small visitor's center and gift shop.

Forty-five minutes west of Tupelo is the town of Oxford, the home of the University of Mississippi, the Center for the Study of Southern Culture, and the University's Blues Archive. Oxford is one of the South's leaders in music and literature—both past and present. At the center of town, Square Books offers browsers one of the finest collections of southern literature in the country. The coffee shop on the bookstore's second floor is a favorite meeting place for university students, literary buffs, and local writers.

Just a short walk from the town square, visitors can stroll among the magnolia trees, pines, and tall cedars that provide shade for Rowan Oak, the stately, white house in which the celebrated author William Faulkner spent much of his adult life. On one wall visitors can see the place where Faulkner, who had run out of paper, once scribbled the outline for one of his novels. Faulkner is buried at the edge of a large, peaceful cemetery not far from Rowan Oak.

Author William Faulkner made his home at Rowan Oak, in Oxford, Mississippi.

THE DELTA

West of Oxford the northern hills gradually empty out into the flat, seemingly endless farmland of the Delta. Much of the Delta is covered by enormous fields of cotton, corn, and soybeans. The distinction between wealth and poverty in the area is startling. Some of the mansions of wealthy planters rise proudly out of the same fields that contain the homes of the workers.

Depending on the season, huge harvesting machines or long, odd-looking irrigation systems can be seen scattered here and there across the fields. During the late harvesting season, the pure, ripe cotton bolls stretch out as far as the eye can see, like a white, fluffy sea against the pale blue, sun-bleached horizon. The region's few trees jut out occasionally from creek beds and marshes and sometimes line the paved entrances to the landowners' homes.

A red harvesting machine harvests fluffy white cotton.

Beside the one-bench railroad stop in the tiny Delta town of Tutwiler, a large plaque commemorates the spot where the great African-American composer W. C. Handy first heard the mournful sound of the blues in 1903. In the years that followed, Handy would incorporate the blues into many of his most popular songs, such as "St. Louis Blues," which introduced people around the world to this vital new form of music. A colorful mural on the opposite side of the railroad tracks, created by local artists Cristen Craven Barnard and Hubert Murphy, depicts the scene in which the well-dressed composer, his hat in his hands, listens attentively to the strange sounds made by a local musician. The mural reads: "In 1903, while touring in the Delta and playing musical engagements, W. C. Handy was waiting for a train in Tutwiler. At the train depot, an unknown musician was singing, while sliding a knife blade down the strings of his guitar. The sound and effect were unforgettable to Handy and became the music known worldwide as 'The Blues.'"

On the back road south of Tutwiler, beside a run-down, wood-framed church, is the grave of the great blues singer and harmonica player Aleck Miller, popularly known as Sonny Boy Williamson. Williamson's tombstone is at the back of a tiny, overgrown cemetery. The rusty harmonicas that litter the grave site were left as tributes by blues fans and aspiring musicians.

Near the center of the Delta the city of Clarksdale is the site of the Delta Blues Museum. The museum contains many rare blues artifacts, including one of B. B. King's original guitars, a steel-bodied acoustic guitar once owned by Son House, and a life-size wax figure of Muddy Waters. The museum is committed to "preserving, protecting and perpetuating the Blues" and often hosts classes taught by local blues musicians in blues history and playing techniques.

VICKSBURG

Perched on high bluffs overlooking the Mississippi River is the historic port city of Vicksburg, the site of the famous Civil War siege and one of the most important battles of the conflict. The city is the home of the largest Civil War cemetery in the United States. The Vicksburg National Military Park preserves the rolling, grass-covered hills and deep ravines where thousands of Union and Confederate soldiers clashed during the bloody battles of General Grant's two-month blockade of the city. Today motorists drive on a 16-mile tour of the battleground, lined by hundreds of statues, monuments, and plaques commemorating battle sites and the various state units that took part in the fighting. Before and after park hours each day, joggers and hikers turn the winding roadway into a popular exercise route and meeting place.

Civil War cannons at Vicksburg National Military Park

WE PUT THE COKE IN THE BOTTLE

In 1894 customers at the Biedenharn Candy Company, in Vicksburg, became the first people in the world to be served Coca-Cola in bottles. Today the site of the original bottling works has been remodeled as the Biedenharn Coca-Cola Museum. The museum features restored bottling equipment from the turn of the century and an old-fashioned soda fountain. Museum visitors can sample both the more syrupy, carbonated Coca-Cola that was popular in the days before bottling and today's recipe in original-size, ice-cold bottles.

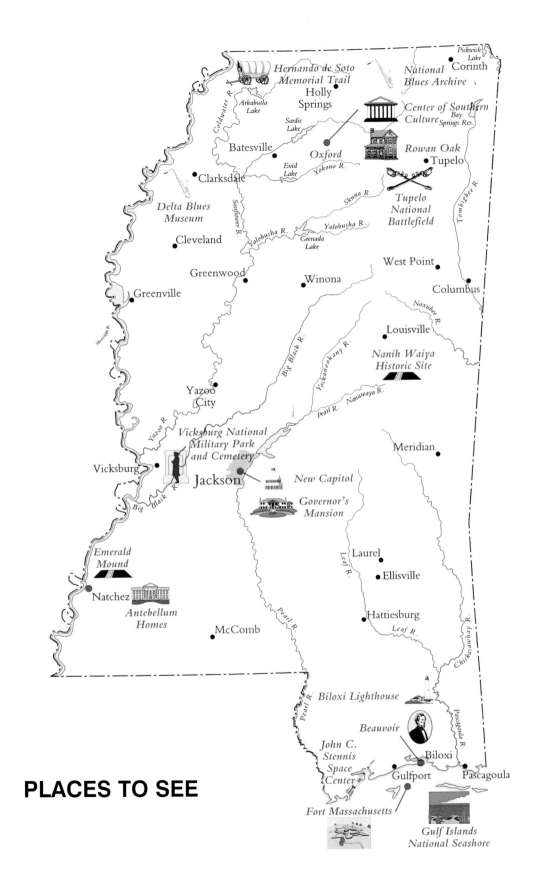

PLACES TO SEE

The largest port city in southwestern Mississippi, Natchez is one of the most beautiful and historically rich cities in the United States. It has more than six hundred pre–Civil War homes—the most of any southern city. More than one hundred of these magnificent structures are registered historic landmarks, and many can be toured by the public. During Christmastime many of Natchez's historic homes are opened to the public. Highlights of the tour include Stanton Hall, a magnificent, white palace with two-story columns that was built in 1857, and Longwood, an octagonal brick home with an Asian-style dome.

A tour of Natchez would not be complete without a visit to Stanton Hall.

Known as the City of Azaleas, Natchez's sidewalks and yards are densely lined with azaleas, magnolias, dogwoods, and other flowering trees and shrubs. For visitors who would prefer not to brave the Mississippi heat on foot, horse-drawn carriages, red double-decker buses, and green and brown trolley cars carry visitors up and down the city's historic stretch.

Down the hill from the antebellum home district is the historic nineteenth-century flatboat and steamboat landing area known as Natchez Under-the-Hill. The hillside offers a spectacular view of the Mississippi River and the dense greenery of the Louisiana countryside across the way.

A few miles north of Natchez, Emerald Mound, the region's largest surviving Indian mound, is a startling sight. Shaped like a pyramid, it is more than 770 feet long and 400 feet wide and covers almost 8 acres of the lush, green countryside.

JACKSON

The capital city of Jackson is a tree-lined community with approximately 200,000 inhabitants. Near the capitol at the center of town, businesspeople and government workers stroll leisurely to and from their offices. People frequently pause to chat with friends on street corners or to drink coffee and read the morning paper in one of the many small diners and cafés. Jackson is one of the Deep South's centers of art, architecture, health care, and education.

At the center of town several of the state's finest buildings are scattered along a six-block stretch. Modeled after the national capitol in Washington, D.C., the state capitol—called the New Capitol—is a huge, three-story brick structure. The New Capitol's tall, white columns rise proudly above the arched doorways on the first floor. Only a few blocks away, its well-preserved predecessor, the Old Capitol, is one of America's

Jackson, Mississippi, is the state capital.

finest examples of Greek Revival architecture. A striking white building, the Old Capitol is made entirely of limestone, granite, and marble. A majestic golden eagle sits atop its massive copper dome. Since the early 1960s it has served as a state historical museum. The building suffered damage in storms that followed Hurricane Katrina.

Not far from the capitol, Hal and Mal's, a popular rib house, offers a glimpse of another side of Jackson. Each night young people crowd into the building to hear the South's leading blues, rhythm-and-blues, and rock-and-roll musicians. All along the restaurant's walls are signed photographs of respected blues musicians—such as B. B. King, Muddy Waters, and John

Lee Hooker—who played at the club in the past. "It's just great to see young people coming out together to this music," says the manager Malcolm White. "That's why I do this. We're known for the blues here, but, the truth is, we get every kind of music. People down here really love their music."

REMEMBERING MEDGAR EVERS

Away from Jackson's downtown, the Medgar Evers Home is now open to the public as a historical landmark. Located in a low-income, predominantly African-American neighborhood on the outskirts of town, the home is where the respected civil rights leader was assassinated by Byron De La Beckwith on June 12, 1963.

In the same part of Jackson, on nearby Medgar Evers Boulevard, is the Medgar Evers Memorial Statue. The 500-pound, cast-bronze statue shows Evers standing with his arms crossed, in a hopeful but defiant position. It is a familiar posture for those who knew the man. "That's Medgar all right," an older African-American man explained to his young grandson as they approached the statue. In the statue, Evers is looking east toward Jackson, the city in which he fought stubbornly and courageously for equal rights and opportunities for African Americans. The inscription at the base of the statue presents a simple message:

Dedicated to Everyone
Who Believes in Peace
Love and Non-Violence
Let's Keep the Torch Burning

TEN LARGEST CITIES

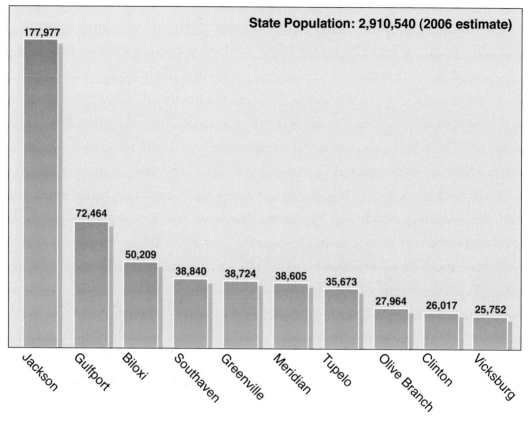

State Population: 2,910,540 (2006 estimate)

City	Population
Jackson	177,977
Gulfport	72,464
Biloxi	50,209
Southaven	38,840
Greenville	38,724
Meridian	38,605
Tupelo	35,673
Olive Branch	27,964
Clinton	26,017
Vicksburg	25,752

MERIDIAN

Meridian is the largest city in the eastern part of the state. The city was once an important railroad center for the Deep South, serving as a hub for train traffic to and from the industrial and tourist centers of the South, such as Memphis, Birmingham, New Orleans, Atlanta, and Mobile.

At Highland Park in Meridian, the Jimmie Rodgers Museum allows visitors a chance to learn more about the life and the music of the Father of Country Music and the railroad era that he memorialized in song. In addition to the singer's guitar and the furniture from his home, the museum also boasts an entire steam engine.

Even though the Gulf Coast suffered great destruction from Hurricane Katrina, within a year the bright neon lights of gambling casinos and high-rise hotels again dominated Mississippi's coastline. Despite the area's recent devastation, the Gulf Coast is still the site of some of the state's most enduring symbols of the Confederacy and the Old South. Fort Massachusetts, completed just after the Civil War, is preserved as a war memorial on West Ship Island, off the shore of Gulfport. The Biloxi Lighthouse, built in 1848, has survived the Civil War and killer hurricanes. After Hurricane Katrina it became a symbol of Mississippi's recovery, standing where it has for years—in the middle of the four-lane Highway 90, which runs along the shore.

The area's most frequently visited historical landmark is Beauvoir, the pre–Civil War house where the Confederate president, Jefferson Davis, spent his last years. The house and grounds suffered great destruction from Hurricane Katrina. Most of the furnishings were immediately picked up and preserved, and work began on restoring the house. Beauvoir should be open to visitors again by the summer of 2008.

As a result of Katrina, Biloxi has a new landmark—the Katrina Memorial. Standing on the Town Green just off Highway 90, the memorial is 12 feet tall—the height of the storm surge. On the wall of the memorial is a tile inlay of a wave. A glass case contains items that were destroyed during the hurricane.

Built in 1848, the Biloxi Lighthouse is reported to be the first metal lighthouse in the South.

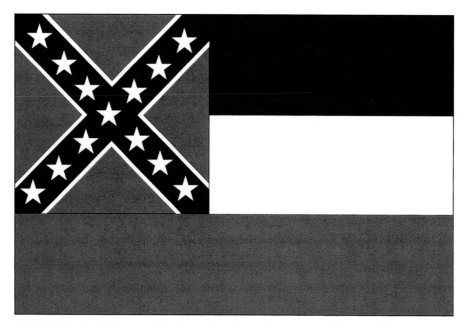

THE FLAG: The state flag has three broad, horizontal bars of blue, white, and red. In the upper left-hand corner is the Confederate flag and a blue cross outlined in white with thirteen stars, all on a red background. The flag was adopted in 1894.

THE SEAL: Adopted in 1798, the state seal features an eagle with outstretched wings. It holds an olive branch in its right talon and three arrows in its left. Encircling the seal are the words "The Great Seal of the State of Mississippi."

State Survey

Statehood: December 10, 1817

Origin of Name: From the Native-American word *misi-sipi*, meaning "big river" or "father of waters"

Nickname: Magnolia State

Capital: Jackson

Motto: By Valor and Arms

Bird: Mockingbird

Waterfowl: Wood duck

Land Mammal: White-tailed deer

Water Mammal: Bottlenose dolphin

Fish: Largemouth or black bass

Flower: Magnolia

Wildflower: Coreopsis

Tree: Magnolia

Insect: Honeybee

Wood duck

Magnolia

GO, MISSISSIPPI

"Go, Mississippi" was adopted as the official song of the Magnolia State by the legislature on May 17, 1962. The words and music were written by Houston Davis.

By Houston Davis

Go, Mis - si - sip - pi, keep roll - ing a - long,

Go, Mis - sis - sip - pi, you can - not go wrong.

Go, Mis - sis - sip - pi, we're sing - ing your song:

M - I - S, - S - I - S, - S - I - P - P - I.

Highest Point: 806 feet above sea level, at Woodall Mountain

Lowest Point: Sea level, along the Gulf of Mexico

Area: 47,695 square miles

Greatest Distance North to South: 331 miles

Great Distance East to West: 208 miles

Bordering States: Alabama to the east, Tennessee to the north, Arkansas and Louisiana to the west

Hottest Recorded Temperature: 115 ºF at Holly Springs on July 29, 1930

Coldest Recorded Temperature: −19 ºF at Corinth on January 30, 1966

Average Annual Precipitation: 56 inches

Major Rivers: Big Black, Chickasawhay, Coldwater, Leaf, Mississippi, Pascagoula, Pearl, Tallahatchie, Tombigbee, Yazoo

Major Lakes: Arkabutla, Columbus, Enid, Grenada, Okatibbee, Pickwick, Ross Barnett, Sardis

Trees: Black oak, cottonwood, cypress, hickory, live oak, magnolia, pecan, pine, red oak, tupelo, walnut

Wild Plants: azalea, black-eyed Susan, camellia, crepe myrtle, dogwood, kudzu, redbud, violet, Spanish moss, Virginia creeper

Animals: black bear, bobcat, coyote, fox, opossum, rabbit, raccoon, squirrel, white-tailed deer, woodchuck

Birds: duck, goose, mockingbird, mourning dove, quail, wild turkey

Fish: bream, catfish, crabs, crappies, flounder, largemouth bass, mackerel, marlin, menhaden, mullet, oysters, perch, redfish, shrimp

Endangered Animals: Amphibians—river frog, Mississippi gopher frog. Reptiles—pine woods snake, mimic glass lizard, black pine snake, hawksbill sea turtle, Kemp's ridley sea turtle, leatherback sea turtle. Fish—Gulf sturgeon, pallid sturgeon, Alabama shad, crystal darter, Yazoo darter, bayou darter. Crayfish and mussels—Choctaw rivulet crayfish, Jackson prairie crayfish, Mississippi flatwoods crayfish, pearl blackwater crayfish, mucket mussel, purple wartyback mussel, Louisiana fatmucket. Birds—brown pelican, Mississippi sandhill crane, southeastern snowy plover, yellow rail, southeastern American kestrel, and American oystercatcher, red-cockaded woodpecker. Mammals—Louisiana black bear, southeastern bat

Endangered Plants: American chaffseed, Southern spicebush, Louisiana quillwort

Brown pelican

Mississippi History

1540 Spanish explorer Hernando de Soto is the first European to reach Mississippi.

1682 René-Robert Cavelier, sieur de la Salle, claims Mississippi for France.

1699 Pierre Le Moyne, Sieur d'Iberville, of France establishes Fort Maurepas at Old Biloxi, the first European settlement in Mississippi.

1719 The French bring the first African slaves to Mississippi to work on rice and tobacco plantations.

1763 As a result of its victory in the French and Indian War, Britain acquires Mississippi from France.

1798 The Mississippi Territory is created, with Natchez as its capital.

1806 A new variety of cotton is introduced to Mississippi from Mexico, beginning the Great Cotton Era.

1817 Mississippi becomes the twentieth state.

1821 The state capital moves to Jackson.

1830 Choctaw Indians sign the Dancing Rabbit Creek Treaty, giving up their lands in Mississippi.

1861 Mississippi secedes from the Union as the Civil War begins; Jefferson Davis, a former U.S. senator from Mississippi, becomes president of the Confederacy.

1863 General Ulysses S. Grant captures Vicksburg during the Civil War, giving the North control of the Mississippi River and splitting the Confederacy in two.

1868 A new state constitution gives African Americans in Mississippi the right to vote and to hold elected office.

1870 Mississippi is readmitted to the Union.

1871 The state opens Alcorn University, the first state-supported college for African Americans in the United States.

1890 Mississippi adopts a new state constitution that takes away many of the rights given to African Americans in the previous constitution.

1926 The state becomes one of the first to ban the teaching of evolution in its public schools.

1939 Oil is discovered in Yazoo County, marking the beginning of the oil industry in Mississippi.

1949 Mississippian William Faulkner wins the Nobel Prize for literature.

1962 Despite protests and riots, James Meredith becomes the first African-American student at the University of Mississippi; federal troops arrive in Mississippi to maintain order.

1963 Civil rights leader Medgar Evers is assassinated at his home in Jackson.

1964 New federal civil rights laws force Mississippi to integrate its public schools.

1973 Eudora Welty wins the Pulitzer Prize in fiction for her novel *The Optimist's Daughter.*

1986 Mike Espy is the first African American elected to the U.S. House of Representatives from Mississippi.

1988 Eugene Marino, a native of Biloxi, becomes the first African-American Roman Catholic archbishop in the United States.

1991 Kirk Fordice becomes Mississippi's first Republican governor since the end of the Civil War.

1997 Mississippi becomes the first state to win lawsuits against tobacco companies.

2005 Hurricane Katrina hits the Gulf Coast, leaving at least 230 dead in Mississippi.

ECONOMY

Agricultural Products: beef, catfish, cotton, eggs, milk, poultry, rice, soybeans

Manufactured Products: appliances, bricks, chemicals, clothing, electronic equipment, fertilizers, paper, processed foods, ships, wood products

Natural Resources: bauxite, limestone, lumber, natural gas, oil, salt

Business and Trade: banking, insurance, investment securities, public finance, retail sales, tourism

Cotton

Martin Luther King Day On Martin Luther King Day, in January, towns throughout the state host parades, lectures, seminars, and other activities to honor the memory of the great civil rights leader.

Dixie National Rodeo and Livestock Show This is the second-largest livestock show and the largest rodeo east of the Mississippi River. Held each February in Jackson, it features livestock competitions, rodeo events, dances, and a parade.

Mardi Gras Parades and Balls Each year before the beginning of Lent, the period before Easter, the people of Biloxi and other Gulf Coast towns celebrate Mardi Gras with music, parades, costume balls, and other festivities.

Mardi Gras Parade

Natchez Powwow At the end of March, Native Americans from around the United States gather in Natchez to celebrate their heritage. Activities include dancing, music, and crafts demonstrations.

Vicksburg Spring Pilgrimage In March and April visitors to Vicksburg get a chance to visit beautiful homes built before the Civil War. People can tour the houses and their gardens and take riverboat rides on the Mississippi to relive a bygone era.

Natchez Spring Pilgrimage Held in March and April in Natchez, this event celebrates the history and beauty of pre–Civil War Mississippi. The monthlong celebration features tours of thirty-one antebellum houses and gardens.

Natchez Spring Pilgrimage

World Catfish Festival In April, Belzoni holds the world's largest catfish fry. Other activities include arts-and-crafts exhibits, music and dancing, and the crowning of the Catfish Queen.

Natchez Festival of Music In May music lovers flock to Natchez to hear performances of operas, Broadway show tunes, and jazz.

Blessing of the Fleet This colorful event, held in Biloxi each May, celebrates the beginning of the fishing season. Fishermen gather their boats in the harbor to receive a religious blessing before venturing out into the Gulf of Mexico.

USA International Ballet Competition Founded in Jackson in 1979, this competition is now held every four years over two weeks in June and July. Dancers come from around the world to compete for medals and cash prizes. Representatives from ballet companies as well as the public watch the competitions.

Fireworks Extravaganza This Fourth of July celebration at Robinsonville features one of the largest fireworks displays in the Southeast.

Neshoba County Fair Held in late July or early August and known as Mississippi's Giant House Party, this annual fair has been celebrated since 1889. One of the last remaining old-style county fairs in the South, it features dancing, singing, harness racing, and other types of entertainment.

Mississippi State Fair Held in Jackson each October, this state fair is the largest in the South. In addition to traditional livestock shows, the fair offers educational demonstrations, art exhibits, entertainment, and carnival rides.

Tennessee Williams Festival On the second weekend in October, Clarksdale hosts this festival. Visitors can attend performances of Williams's plays, listen to lectures about his writing, and tour his boyhood home.

Christmas on the Water In early December, Biloxi starts the Christmas season with an evening parade of lighted boats followed by fireworks. A children's parade is also part of the festivities.

STATE STARS

Blanche Kelso Bruce (1841–1898), was the second African American to serve in the U.S. Senate. Bruce was born in Virginia and moved to Mississippi in 1869. In 1874 he was elected to the U.S. Senate, where he devoted much of his time to fighting corruption and promoting better race relations. After leaving the Senate, Bruce served in the U.S. Treasury Department.

Bo Diddley (1928–   ), a well-known rhythm-and-blues singer, was born Ellas Bates in McComb. A self-taught musician, the African-American singer gained fame for the driving tempo of his music. A pioneer of the electric guitar, he became one of the first rock-and-roll stars, with songs such as "Who Do You Love?"

Bo Diddley

Medgar Evers (1925–1963), born in Decatur, was one of the best-known civil rights leaders of the 1950s and early 1960s. He joined the National Association for the Advancement of Colored People (NAACP) in 1952 and later became the secretary of the organization in Mississippi. He played an important role in the struggle to end segregation in Mississippi, giving fiery speeches about the rights of African Americans. Because of his outspoken position, Evers became a target for civil rights opponents. In 1963 he was assassinated by Byron De La Beckwith.

William Faulkner (1897–1962), one of the greatest American writers of the twentieth century, was born in New Albany. Faulkner spent most of his career in Mississippi writing about the South. In his books, which reflect the color and history of the region, he explores love, bravery, and endurance. Faulkner won the Nobel Prize for literature in 1949 and the Pulitzer Prize in 1955 and 1963 for his novels *A Fable* and *The Reivers*.

Brett Favre (1969–   ), the quarterback for the Green Bay Packers football team (1992–   ), was born in Kiln. As a young boy he bragged that he would quarterback in a Super Bowl and win. Favre was a star athlete at the University of Southern Mississippi before joining the National Football League. As a Packer he has won three NFL Most Valuable Player awards. In 1997 Favre fulfilled his prediction and led the Packers to a Super Bowl victory.

John Grisham (1955–   ), a popular novelist, was born in Arkansas but grew up in Mississippi. Originally a lawyer, Grisham was inspired to write by a trial he watched in 1984. His first novel, *A Time to Kill*, got good reviews but sold few copies. However, his next novel, *The Firm*, became a best seller and launched his career. Many of his books have been made into movies, including *The Firm*, *The Pelican Brief*, and *The Client*.

Fannie Lou Hamer (1917–1977), a civil rights leader, was born to sharecroppers in Montgomery County. She became active in the civil rights movement, organizing protests, leading voter-registration drives, and working to reform the Democratic Party so that African Americans were treated fairly.

Beth Henley (1952–), a playwright, was born in Jackson. Henley is best known for her witty comedies and emotional dramas that highlight the atmosphere of the South. Henley first pursued a career in acting, but she turned to writing plays after discovering that there were not many good roles for southern women. Her first play, *Crimes of the Heart*, won a Tony Award and a Pulitzer Prize in 1981.

Jim Henson (1936–1990), the creator of the Muppets, was born in Greenville. Henson began working as a puppeteer, but he really wanted a career in television. In 1955 his puppet creations appeared on a local television station in Maryland. In 1969 Henson and his Muppets became a household name, when *Sesame Street* first appeared on television. The Muppets—including Big Bird, Bert, Ernie, Miss Piggy, and Kermit the Frog—became the beloved friends of millions of kids around the world.

Jim Henson

Robert Johnson (1911–1938), one of the greatest Mississippi blues musicians, was born in Hazlehurst and grew up in Robinsonville. During his short life he developed an extraordinary talent playing blues guitar and helped define the blues as an art form. Johnson recorded many blues songs, including "Crossroad Blues" and

"Hellbound on My Trail." His songs voiced his anger and the suffering he experienced in his life.

James Earl Jones (1931–), a well-known African-American actor, was born in Arkabutla. Best known for his deep, rumbling voice, Jones has appeared in many movies and on television. In one of his most famous roles, he did not even appear onscreen but was the voice of Darth Vader in the Star Wars movies. He also appeared in the television miniseries *Roots* and in the movie *Field of Dreams*. A stage actor as well, Jones won a Tony Award in 1969 for his role in *The Great White Hope*.

Florence Latimer Mars (1923–2006), an outspoken white civil rights worker, was born in Philadelphia. She spoke out against the Ku Klux Klan and other groups that oppressed Mississippi's black population. Her 1977 book *Witness in Philadelphia* told about the effects on her hometown of the 1964 killings of three civil rights workers—Andrew Goodman, Michael Schwerner, and James Earl Chaney. In 2005 she finally witnessed the conviction and sentencing of Edgar Ray Killen for the 1964 murders.

James Meredith (1933–), born in Kosciusko, gained fame in 1962 as the first African American to attend the University of Mississippi. In 1966 he led a civil rights march from Memphis, Tennessee, to Jackson, Mississippi, to encourage African Americans to register to vote. During the march Meredith was shot and wounded, but he rejoined the march after recovering from his wounds. He ran unsuccessfully for the U.S. Senate in 1972.

Brandy Norwood (1979–), born in McComb, is better known as Brandy. The popular singer and actress recorded her first album at age fourteen. Two singles from that album, "I Wanna Be Down" and "Baby," became hits. Her singing style combines rhythm and blues, gospel, and soul music. In 1993 she landed a role on the television program *Thea* and went on to star in the show *Moesha*, which premiered in 1995.

Brandy Norwood

Walter Payton (1954–1999), born in Columbia, was one of the greatest running backs in football history. After being named an All-American at Jackson State University, he began his professional career with the Chicago Bears in 1975. He led the NFL in rushing every year from 1975 to 1979 and was named player of the year in 1977. Payton helped lead the Bears to a Super Bowl victory in 1986. He retired in 1987.

Elvis Presley (1935–1977), one of the great legends of American music, was born in Tupelo. The singer combined country and western with rhythm and blues to help define the new sound of rock and roll. Songs such as "Heartbreak Hotel," "Love Me Tender," and "Don't Be Cruel" made him one of the most popular performers of the 1950s and 1960s. Although his life was cut short, his music and popularity have endured.

Leontyne Price (1927–   ), one of the world's most famous African-American opera singers, was born in Laurel. The soprano has sung in most of the major opera houses of the world, including the Metropolitan Opera in New York City. She is best known for her dramatic roles in such operas as *Aida* and *Il Trovatore*. Now retired from the stage, Price still gives occasional recitals and teaches. During her career she won fifteen Grammy awards.

Charley Pride (1938–   ), the first well-known African-American country singer, was born on a cotton plantation in Sledge. As a young man Pride taught himself to play guitar but hoped for a career in professional baseball. After playing in the minor leagues for about ten years, he decided to become a singer and set out for Nashville, where his initial success came after appearances at the Grand Ole Opry.

Pushmataha (1765?–1824), a Choctaw chief, was born near Noxuba Creek. In the early 1800s he began working to ensure peace between his tribe and the U.S. government. In 1805 Pushmataha signed a treaty that allowed white settlement on Choctaw land. Later, he persuaded his tribe to join the United States in fighting against the Creek Indians during the Creek War. In 1816 and 1820 he signed other agreements with the U.S. government, giving away more of the Indians' lands.

Pushmataha

Hiram Rhoades Revels (1827–1901), though born in North Carolina, served Mississippi as the first African-American member of the U.S. Senate. He settled in Natchez in 1866 and was elected to the state senate. In 1870 he was chosen to fill an unexpired term in the U.S. Senate. As a senator, Revels sought to improve educational opportunities for African Americans. He served only one term and then became the president of Alcorn University in Mississippi, a college for African Americans.

Jerry Rice (1962–   ), a professional football player, was born in Starkville. An All-American at Mississippi Valley State, Rice joined the San Francisco 49ers in 1985. He soon earned a reputation as the best wide receiver in professional football. He led the league in yardage and touchdowns in 1986 and set many records in the following years. Rice played with the 49ers in two Super Bowl championships and was named Most Valuable Player in the 1989 game.

Pearl Rivers (1849–1896), born Eliza Jane Poitevent in Hancock County, was the first woman publisher of an important daily newspaper. Writing under the name Pearl Rivers, she became an editor of the *New Orleans Times-Picayune* in 1870. She married the owner of the paper and managed it herself after his death, in 1896, adding sections for women, such as fashion and household tips, and a society page.

Jimmie Rodgers (1897–1933), known as the Father of Country Music, was born in Meridian. He taught himself to play the guitar and banjo and developed a singing style that combined country, blues, and cowboy music. Rodgers became a popular recording artist and toured throughout the South. His songs, including such hits as "Brakeman's Blues" and "Mississippi River Blues," had a great influence on other singers.

Conway Twitty (1933–1993), a country singer and guitarist, was born in Friars Point with the name Harold Jenkins. Twitty made his first radio appearance at age ten. He recorded his first hits, including "I Need Your Lovin'," in 1958. Starting in the 1970s, Twitty appeared regularly at the Grand Ole Opry, often paired with the singer Loretta Lynn.

Muddy Waters (1915–1983), a legendary African-American blues singer, was born McKinley Morganfield in Rolling Fork. He began his professional singing career in 1943, after moving to Chicago, and became known as King of the Chicago Blues. His unique style, which sounded like moaning and shouting, influenced many rhythm-and-blues bands, especially in England. One of his songs, "Rollin' Stone," served as the inspiration for the English group the Rolling Stones.

Ida Bell Wells (1862–1931), a journalist, was born to enslaved parents in Holly Springs. Wells taught in rural schools before becoming a journalist in the 1880s. In 1892 Wells began a crusade to stop lynching in the South, traveling throughout the United States and England, speaking to antilynching societies. In 1910 she founded the Chicago Negro Fellowship League, which helped African Americans who had migrated from the South. She also played a role in founding the NAACP.

Eudora Welty (1909–2001), a well-known writer, was born in Jackson. Throughout her career Welty's work focused on Mississippi and its people. Her writings paint a colorful and vibrant portrait of life in the South. In the 1930s Welty had essays published in literary reviews. Some short stories, published in the 1940s, brought her great success. She won a Pulitzer Prize in 1973 for her novel *The Optimist's Daughter.*

Eudora Welty

Tennessee Williams (1911–1983), one of America's greatest playwrights, was born Thomas Lanier Williams in Columbus. In 1938 he went to New Orleans and began using the name "Tennessee" on stories he wrote for magazines. He first gained fame as a playwright in the 1940s and won a Pulitzer Prize in 1948 and in 1955 for his plays *A Streetcar Named Desire* and *Cat on a Hot Tin Roof.* His works—noted for their realism, intense emotions, and use of symbolism—are classics of the theater.

Oprah Winfrey (1954–   ), a popular talk-show host, was born in Kosciusko. After winning two beauty pageants, she went to college at Tennessee State University and then landed a job on a local television news program. In 1983 she got her own morning talk show on a local Chicago station. Two years later she gained national recognition for her role in the movie *The Color Purple*. The next year her talk show went national, and before long *The Oprah Winfrey Show* had become the most-watched daytime talk show in America.

Oprah Winfrey

Richard Wright (1908–1960), a novelist, was born near Natchez. The son of a sharecropper, he first gained fame in 1938 for a collection of short stories called *Uncle Tom's Children*. His writings deal mainly with the struggles of African Americans in a racist society. His best-known novel, *Native Son*, won acclaim for its realism and power. His autobiography, *Black Boy*, captures the pain, fear, pleasures, and hopes that he experienced during his childhood in the South. From 1947 until his death, Wright lived in France because he experienced less racial prejudice there.

Tammy Wynette (1942–1998), born in Tupelo, was a popular country-music star. She taught herself to play piano and guitar and worked in various jobs before heading to Nashville to break into the country-music scene. A regular performer with the Grand Ole Opry beginning in 1969, she had many successful songs, including "Stand By Your Man."

Beauvoir (Biloxi) This pre–Civil War mansion was the retirement home of the Confederate president, Jefferson Davis. The home's name means "beautiful view" because the home faces the Gulf of Mexico. Although severely damaged by Hurricane Katrina, Beauvoir is being restored to its former glory and will reopen again for tours in 2008.

Vicksburg National Military Park (Vicksburg) This park preserves trenches, rifle pits, a Confederate cemetery, and other reminders of the siege of Vicksburg during the Civil War.

Natchez Trace Parkway (Natchez to Nashville) The scenic roadway that runs between Natchez, Mississippi, and Nashville, Tennessee, follows an ancient trading path established by Native Americans and used later by white settlers. Along the roadway are picnic sites, nature trails, museums, historic sites, and early Native American mounds.

Mississippi Petrified Forest (Flora) The only petrified forest in the eastern United States, this site contains giant fossilized trees dating from about 36 million years ago. Visitors can wander nature trails, visit a museum devoted to the geology of the region, and browse in the rock and gem shop.

Delta Blues Museum (Clarksdale) This fascinating museum honors the blues music of the South, bringing the music and its performers to life with videos, recordings, photographs, slide shows, and memorabilia.

French Camp Historic Area (French Camp) This restored settlement from the early 1800s features a log cabin and the pre–Civil War home of a Confederate officer. Visitors can view exhibits and watch craft demonstrations and the operation of a grain mill.

Rainwater Observatory and Planetarium (French Camp) This observatory, the largest in Mississippi, provides public access to sixteen working telescopes. The observatory also features models of the solar system, astronomy exhibits, and a planetarium that offers daily sky shows.

Cottonlandia Museum (Greenwood) Exhibits telling the story of the Delta's cotton industry are housed in this museum. In addition, art and artifacts, including Native American beadwork and arrowheads, present the history of the Delta and its early people.

Choctaw Museum of the Southern Indian (Choctaw) Located on the Choctaw Indian Reservation, this museum contains exhibits on the life and culture of the Choctaw Indians and other southeastern Native American tribes.

Emerald Mound (Natchez) The second-largest Indian ceremonial mound in the nation, Emerald Mound covers almost 8 acres. It is thought to have been built around 1400. A trail leads to the top of the mound, which offers spectacular views of the surrounding area.

Emerald Mound

Mount Locust Inn (Natchez) Built around 1780, this is the only remaining example of a frontier inn, called a stand, on the Natchez Trace. Restored to its original appearance, the inn gives visitors a glimpse of the accommodations available to travelers on the frontier in the late 1700s and early 1800s.

Stennis Space Center (Nicholson) Used to test systems for the space shuttle and experimental spacecraft, this center is NASA's second-largest field installation. A visitors center provides a look at the U.S.

space program and its astronauts. The center is named for John C. Stennis, a former U.S. senator from Mississippi.

Dunn's Falls Water Park (Enterprise) This park features a 65-foot waterfall that was once used to power a historic gristmill. It also offers a wildlife refuge, picnic areas, swimming areas, and hiking trails.

Old Number One Firehouse Museum (Greenville) This firehouse is now a museum that features hands-on displays about firefighting, an area where children can dress up in period costumes, and a big 1927 fire engine named Bertha.

Birthplace of Kermit the Frog Exhibit (Leland) Built to commemorate the Mississippian Jim Henson, this exhibit displays the original Muppets, including Kermit the Frog. There are also videos of early Henson television shows and Muppet memorabilia.

Scott Aquarium (Biloxi) Located on the campus of the Gulf Coast Research Laboratory, the center features more than forty large aquariums filled with local sea creatures and plant life. Part of the aquarium was relocated to Ocean Springs because of damage caused by Hurricane Katrina.

Hattiesburg Zoo (Hattiesburg) One of the best small zoos in the South lets visitors take a train ride on a scale-model railroad through acres of animal exhibits. The zoo also has educational programs and an animal hospital.

Mississippi is the final resting place of royalty. Rose Hill Cemetery in Meridian contains the graves of Emil and Kelly Mitchell, the king and queen of the Gypsies (now called Roma) in the United States. Since 1915, Roma from around the nation have visited the grave to leave small gifts in honor of their royal family.

Although it may never have really rained cats and dogs, strange things do fall from the sky. On May 11, 1887, during a severe hailstorm near Bovina, a large hailstone fell from the sky. Inside the 6-by-8-inch hailstone was a small gopher turtle, completely encased in the ice.

While hunting near Onward, Mississippi, in 1901, President Theodore Roosevelt refused to shoot a small, exhausted bear he came upon in the woods. Soon after that a New Yorker named Morris Michtom designed a stuffed toy bear in honor of the president's action. He called this stuffed bear "Teddy's Bear," which marked the beginning of teddy bears in America.

If people can sing, why not rivers? The Singing River in Pascagoula is famous for the music it makes, which sounds like a swarm of bees. According to legend the music is the song of two Native Americans who drowned themselves in the river rather than marry others chosen by their families.

Find Out More

If you'd like to find out more about Mississippi, look for the following titles in your library, bookstore, or video store, or on the Internet.

BOOKS

Somervill, Barbara A. *Mississippi.* (Sea to Shining Sea). Danbury, CT: Children's Press, 2003.

McMullan, Margaret. *How I Found the Strong.* Boston: Houghton Mifflin Company, 2004.

Shangle, Robert D., ed. *The Wrath of Hurricane Katrina: One of the World's Worst Natural Disasters.* Beaverton, OR: American Products Publishing Company, 2005.

AUDIO RECORDINGS

Hooker, John Lee. *The Ultimate Collection (1948-1990).* Rhino.

Howlin' Wolf. *The Chess Box.* Chess MCA.

Johnson, Robert. *King of the Delta Blues.* Columbia.

Presley, Elvis. *The Sun Sessions.* RCA.

Waters, Muddy. *Folk Singer.* Chess MCA.

VIDEOS

Katrina: South Mississippi's Story. Feature Films Studio, 2005. DVD, two-disk set, with more than six hours of footage compiled by WLOX, southern Mississippi's TV station.

Mississippi State Secrets. A&E Home Video, 2006. Produced by the History Channel, this DVD exposes how the State of Mississippi spied from 1959 to 1972 on people connected to the civil rights movement.

Struggle for Vicksburg. Finley-Holiday Film Corp., 2002. This ninety minute DVD blends photographs of Vicksburg National Battlefield with authentic illustrations from the actual battle. Extras include a quiz, music video, and historical film of salvaging the gunboat *Cairo*.

WEB SITES

Delta Blues Museum
http://www.deltabluesmuseum.org
This Web site has pages about the history of the blues; biographies of blues singers, composers, and musicians; and a calendar of events and exhibits.

Mississippi Division of Tourism
http://www.visitmississippi.org
This tourism-related Web site has information about attractions, events, and festivals throughout the state.

The Official State Web Site of Mississippi
http://www.state.ms.us
This detailed Web site presents information about Mississippi government and related agencies, along with a thorough list of other Mississippi Web sites and up-to-date news headlines about the state.

Index

Page numbers in **boldface** are illustrations and charts.

David Shirley grew up in Tupelo, Mississippi, and attended Mississippi College. His many books for young people include a biography of the Mississippi blues legend B. B. King and a history of rock and roll. He has also written for such magazines as *Rolling Stone*. Although he now lives in Brooklyn, New York, he returns to Mississippi often to visit family and friends.

Patricia K. Kummer received a B.A. degree in history from the College of St. Catherine in St. Paul, Minnesota, and an M.A. degree in history from Marquette University in Milwaukee, Wisconsin. She has written more than fifty books about states, countries, inventions, and other topics. Growing up, Kummer heard many stories about Mississippi from her father and mother. They had lived in Biloxi when her father was stationed at Keesler Air Force Base during World War II. Since the 1990s Kummer has enjoyed visiting Mississippi several times. She lives in Lisle, Illinois, with her husband and enjoys spending time with their grown children and young granddaughters, as well as traveling.